PASSION, POISON AND POWER

THE MYSTERIOUS DEATH OF SIR THOMAS OVERBURY

A Jacobean Mystery
in Fourteen Acts

Sir Thomas Overbury

PASSION, POISON AND POWER

THE MYSTERIOUS DEATH OF SIR THOMAS OVERBURY

A Jacobean Mystery
in Fourteen Acts

BRIAN HARRIS QC

*'Take heed ye princes by examples past
Blood will have blood, either first or last.'*

This quotation from *The Mirror for Magistrates* (1559)
was found on notes prepared by Sir Edward Coke,
principal investigator of the Overbury affair.

WS&H

Wildy, Simmonds & Hill Publishing

Copyright © 2010 Brian Harris

Passion, Poison and Power. The Mysterious Death of Sir Thomas Overbury. A Jacobean Mystery in Fourteen Acts

Frontispiece © TopFoto

British Library Cataloguing in Publication Data

A catalogue record for this book is available from the British Library

ISBN 9780854900770

Printed and bound in the United Kingdom by Antony Rowe Ltd, Chippenham, Wiltshire

The right of Brian Harris QC to be identified as the Author of this Work has been asserted by him in accordance with Copyright, Designs and Patents Act 1988, sections 77 and 78.

All rights reserved. No part of this book may be reproduced, stored in a retrieval system, or transmitted, in any form or by any means, electronic, mechanical, photocopying, recording or otherwise, without the consent of the copyright owners, application for which should be addressed to the publisher. Such a written permission must also be obtained before any part of this publication is stored in a retrieval system of any nature.

Other books by Brian Harris include *Injustice* (Sutton Publishing, 2006) and *Intolerance* (Wildy, Simmonds & Hill, 2008)

First published in 2010 by
Wildy, Simmonds & Hill Publishing
58 Carey Street
London WC2A 2JF
England

In memory of
Stephen

Acknowledgements

I am grateful to Gill Gibbins, David Mees and John Spencer for reading and commenting so thoughtfully on the text of this book, to David Thomas M.B., Ch.B., M.R.C.G.P. for his advice on the medical issues to which it gives rise and to the Rev. Chris Goble for improving my understanding of old Compton Scorpion.

CONTENTS

Acknowledgements   vi

Characters   ix

Prologue   1

Act 1   The empty stage   3

Act 2   The husband, his wife and her lovers   26

Act 3   The annulment   42

Act 4   Overbury in the Tower   49

Act 5   'The Gallant Masque of Lords'   65

Act 6   A new star rises   76

Act 7   'A net to catch the little fishes'   98

Act 8   The fall of the house of Somerset   123

Act 9   The Somersets on Trial   134

Act 10	Was justice done?	154
Act 11	Was Carr a murderer?	162
Act 12	The conspiracy theories	169
Act 13	Who or what killed Overbury?	179
Act 14	And afterwards	194

Author's note   200
Principal sources   202
Index   205

CHARACTERS

THE ROYAL FAMILY

James Stuart: James VI of Scotland and I of England

Queen Anne of Denmark: wife of James

Henry Frederick Stuart: Prince of Wales and son of King James I

Charles Stuart: second son and heir to King James I

ROYAL OFFICIALS

Sir Robert Cecil: later Lord Salisbury, Principal Secretary to the King

Sir Gervase Elwes: The Lieutenant of the Tower

Sir George More: Lieutenant of the Tower after Elwes

Sir Thomas Monson: Member of Parliament, Master of the Armoury in the Tower of London and a client of Northampton's

William Trumbull: the King's agent in Brussels

Sir William Wade: Lieutenant of the Tower before Elwes

Sir Ralph Winwood: Ambassador to the Hague; later, the King's principal Secretary of State

Sir David Wood: one of the Queen's Scottish servants

THE HOWARD FAMILY

Lady Frances Howard ('Frances'): younger daughter of Thomas Howard and his wife, Katherine Knyvett; wife of Robert Devereux (1606) and Robert Somerset (1613)

Henry Howard: first Earl of Northampton ('Northampton'), great uncle to Frances

Henry Howard: a brother of Frances

Thomas Howard: First Earl of Suffolk, Admiral; father of Frances and nephew of Northampton

Katherine Knyvett: second wife of Thomas Howard

The Essex family

Robert Devereux: son of Elizabeth's courtier executed for treason; restored to the Earldom of Essex by King James; husband of Frances

The King's Favourites (in chronological order)

Esmé Stuart: Sieur d'Aubigny, second cousin to King James; raised to the peerage by James, he became Duke of Lennox on his brother's death in 1624

Philip Herbert: Earl of Montgomery, second son of the Earl of Pembroke; created Baron Herbert of Shurland, and first earl of Montgomery (1605)

Robert Carr ('Carr'): son of Thomas Kerr, Laird of Ferniehirst; created Viscount Rochester (1611); Earl of Somerset and Baron Carr of Bransprath (1613); married Frances in 1613

George Villiers: knighted (1615); created Baron Whaddon of Whaddon and Viscount Villiers (1616); Earl of Buckingham (1617); Marquis (1618); Duke of Buckingham (1623)

Overbury and his circle

Sir Thomas Overbury: knighted (1608)

Sir Robert Bruce Cotton: friend of Overbury; courtier, politician and antiquarian

Sir Robert Killigrew: friend of Overbury

Sir John Lidcote: Overbury's brother in law

Henry Payton: one of Overbury's servants

Giles Rawlins: Carr's manservant and Overbury's cousin

THE JUDGES AND LAWYERS

George Abbot: Archbishop of Canterbury and chairman of the annulment commission

Sir Francis Bacon: Attorney General and Lord Chancellor

Robert Bright: a Middlesex coroner

Sir Edward Coke: Chief Justice

Sir Randolph Crewe: Serjeant at law and Chancellor to the Queen

Lord Ellesmere: Lord Chancellor

Lawrence Hyde: the Queen's Attorney and prosecutor of Weston

Sir Henry Montague: Serjeant at law and Recorder of London

Sir Henry Yelverton: Solicitor General and friend of the Howards

THE MEDICAL MEN

Francis Anthony: a quack physician

Simon Forman: doctor, astrologist and necromancer

Paul de Loubell: Mayerne's dispenser

Theodore de Mayerne: the King's principal physician

James Naismith: Mayerne's assistant and surgeon

William Reeve: Loubell's assistant

ANNE TURNER AND HER CIRCLE

Anne Turner: widowed friend of Frances Howard who lived with Sir Arthur Mainwaring

James Franklin: apothecary who sometimes claimed to be a doctor

Sir Arthur Mainwaring: Anne Turner's partner

Richard Weston: Overbury gaoler and one time employee of Anne Turner

Mary Woods: a practitioner in rural magic known as 'Cunning Mary'

THE WALK-ON PARTS

Sir Dudley Digges: prominent MP

James Hay: Carr's former patron

Ben Jonson: the poet and playwright

Simon Merston: Monson's former employee

Edward Rider: landlord of Loubell's father

John Simcocks: friend of Weston

Sir John Wentworth: a friend of Sir John Lidcote

Sir David Wood: one of the Queen's Scottish servants

Henry Wriothesley: Third Earl of Southampton

PROLOGUE

Little attention was paid at the time to the death in the Tower of London of Sir Thomas Overbury, but two years later six people went to the gallows for his murder in a case which was said to involve wizardry, love potions, coded letters and a poisoned enema. Following them into the dock were the most glamorous couple at the court of King James.

The husband, who was rumoured to be the King's lover, was convicted of Overbury's murder despite his protestations of innocence; but was he actually guilty? His pretty young wife confessed to the murder; but did she actually commit the crime? And the Lord Chief Justice was convinced that the case had a significance far wider and more sinister than appeared on the surface, possibly involving the suspicious death of the Prince of Wales.

It has been said of this strange story that:

'[T]he parties at first thought there was very little hurt. Had they foreseen that train of evils that succeeded that injustice, treachery and ingratitude; the barbarous murder they must commit to conceal the first crime; the many persons there would be a necessity of drawing into the same guilt; the lives that must be lost, and the eternal infamy that must succeed, they would surely never have engaged in such an attempt ...'[1]

---

[1] Thomas Salmon, *A New Abridgement and Critical Review of the State Trials 1388–1736* (Dublin, 1737).

Passion, Poison and Power

    Despite an exhaustive inquiry conducted by England's most feared prosecutor the whole truth never came to light; even the official report of the trials is suspect. Nevertheless, we must do our best to understand the circumstances behind Overbury's terrible death, not just because of the light they throw on a key period of English history, but also out of our need to get to the bottom of the most intriguing murder mystery of the seventeenth century.

ACT 1

THE EMPTY STAGE

Thomas Overbury was born on 18 June 1581 in Compton Scorpion (or Compton Scorfen, as it used to be) near Ilmington in Warwickshire.[2] The tiny hamlet had a long history: it was mentioned in the *Domesday Book* and boasts a lane which in Roman times connected Icknield Street and the Fosse Way. Most of the buildings are made of the soft Cotswold stone. Grandest among them is the manor house just south of the village. Though re-constructed more than once, it still contains features of the original sixteenth-century structure which was occupied by Thomas' parents, the barrister, Nicolas Overbury formerly of Bourton-on-the-Hill in Gloucestershire, and his wife, Mary Palmer. It is difficult to imagine an environment further removed from the glittering court in which young Thomas was to make his name or the grim prison in which he was to end his days.

Thomas was fortunate in that his father was a rich enough landowner to afford to enrol him in The Queen's college, Oxford as a gentleman commoner. He proved to be an enthusiastic scholar and, armed with a Bachelor degree in logic and philosophy, joined his father's Inn of Court, the Middle Temple, at the age of seventeen. At that time the Inns were magnets for poets and

---

[2] He was baptized in the nearby village of Barton-on-the-Heath.

Passion, Poison and Power

writers as much as for lawyers, and, although there is no record of Overbury ever having been called to the Bar, the young man seems to have stood out among his contemporaries.[3] Some time during his studies his father sent him to Edinburgh on 'a voyage of pleasure', accompanied by his chief clerk carrying letters of introduction from an influential friend, the Queen's Secretary of State, Sir Robert Cecil. While he was there an Oxford colleague introduced him to a fourteen-year-old Scot, Robert Kerr who soon became his friend and admirer. The relationship was to become the dominant influence, for good and ill, in both their lives.

Later, when the Scot became famous, some were inclined to dismiss him as a man of no substance or background, but this was far from the case. The Kerrs (or Kers) were an old Scottish family. Some time around 1470 they had built a Peel tower in Ferniehurst, a village just south of Jedburgh in the Border country. It was destroyed a century or so later in the course of one of the interminable disputes that plagued the area and was rebuilt as the imposing castle it is today. Sir Thomas Kerr, Robert's father and laird of Ferniehirst, had supported Mary Queen of Scots during the Northern revolt of 1569, but was pardoned for this later by King James Stuart, at the intervention of his beloved cousin, Esmé. Fifteen years later Thomas was appointed Warden of the Middlemarch, but died later under a cloud, having been arrested for suspected murder. It was at about this time (the date is not known exactly) that Thomas' second wife, Jean, gave birth to their fourth son, Robert. The child's future might have been bleak but for the fact that, some years before, his father had attempted (unsuccessfully) to rescue his King from the rebels who had captured him. The grateful James took the boy to be brought up in his court, where in time he became a page to George Home, later Earl of Dunbar.

---

[3] His *bon mots* were recorded in John Manningham's *Diaries*.

But an event was about to happen which would translate King James, along with Kerr, Overbury, and the rest of his court, out of Edinburgh and into an entirely different environment some hundreds of miles away.

THE DEATH OF THE QUEEN

England's Queen Elizabeth died in 1603 after a long drawn-out illness. As she gradually lost her grip on life so she lost command of her country; what disasters might her death foretell? Fortunately, there was someone at hand to plan for the future, the indispensable Robert Cecil. Cecil, a short, humpbacked man whom Elizabeth described affectionately as her 'pigmy', can claim credit for much of the stability of his mistress' reign. Determined that it should not be thrown away upon her death, he had for some time been conducting negotiations behind Elizabeth's back with her closest relative, the Scottish King with a view to securing the peaceful transfer of power. It was a dangerous enterprise which, if discovered, could have cost him his head. Fortunately for him, it paid off. When the last of the Tudors finally expired, Cecil was able to persuade the Privy Council to offer the throne to James: the offer was promptly and enthusiastically accepted. Leaving his pregnant wife and three children in Edinburgh, James made a stately progress south, stopping on the way to reward an innkeeper with the title to a manor, to create a host of new knights and to hang a cut-purse under the impression that he had power to do so without benefit of trial. No one knew how the English, who for two generations had known only one monarch, would receive another, and from a country with which they had for so long been at odds. To everyone's relief, the new King was universally welcomed, but the transition was not without its difficulties.

James came from a poor and backward land riven by clannish and baronial disputes and religious strife into one which had enjoyed prosperity and internal peace for over a century and which was about to enter the most artistically and commercially prolific period in its history. Even the look of the land was changing, with brick and stone replacing wood and wattle as its building materials. The only remaining threats came from abroad.

Elizabeth's father, Henry VIII, had severed the English church violently from the church of Rome and had to suffer the consequences. Elizabeth continued his policy of discriminating against Catholics and, like her father, was excommunicated for it by the Pope. But she also faced another threat closer to home. Mary Queen of Scots, her first cousin once removed, had long laid claim to the English throne, a claim which not even imprisonment had made her relinquish. Mary's continued plotting to overthrow Elizabeth finally forced her reluctant cousin to consent to her execution. While most English Catholics were content to bask in the national prosperity a significant minority were disaffected. Jesuit priests were being infiltrated into the country at the risk of their lives, while Catholic powers like Spain stood by, alert to exploit England's weaknesses. It was a recipe for revolt.

As part of his campaign to secure the throne, James had thrown out the heaviest of hints that he would relieve followers of 'the old religion' of the restrictions under which they suffered, but failed to live up to his promise when in a position to do so. 'We'll not need the Papists now', he cynically exclaimed. It was not surprising, therefore, that hardly had the new King got on his throne than he was nearly blown off it by a small group of recusants (as Roman Catholics were known) led by Robert Catesby. Called at the time the powder treason, their conspiracy is better known now as the Gunpowder Plot. When Guy Fawkes, the plotters' explosives expert, was asked by his interrogators why he had planned the death of the King and his government he answered, 'To blow the Scottish beggars back to their native mountains'.

But nothing could stop James' determination to enjoy the wealth of his new-found land and stamp it with his character. He started by rewarding his Scottish followers at the expense of the English. He justified this by saying:

> 'Had I been oversparing to them, they might have thought Joseph had forgotten his brethren, or that the king had been drunk with his new kingdom. If I did respect the English when I came first—what might the Scotch have justly said, if I had not in some measure dealt bountifully with them that so long had served me, so far adventured themselves with me, and been so faithful to me?'

Very soon there were eight Scottish gentlemen of the bedchamber for every Englishman. In fact, so extensive was the process of Scottification that it has been said that by 1607 it no longer made sense to talk of an English court.[4]

What sort of man, then, was James Stuart?

JAMES THE MAN

James was a curious mixture, both physically and intellectually. One of his contemporaries left this memorable picture of the man:

> 'He was of a middle stature, more corpulent through his cloathes than in his body, yet fat enough, his cloathes ever being made large and easie, the Doublets quilted for stiletto proof, his Breeches in plates, and full stuffed: He was naturally of a timorous disposition, which was the reason of his quilted doublets, his eye large, ever rowling after any stranger came in his presence, inasmuch, who that for shame have left the room, as being out of countenance; his Beard was very thin; his tongue too large for his mouth, which ever made him drink very uncomely, as if eating his drink, which came out into the cup of each side his mouth; his skin was

---

[4] Keith M. Brown, 'The Scottish Aristocracy, Anglicization and the Court, 1603-38', *The Historical Journal*, Vol. 36, No. 3, September 1993, pp. 543–76.

as soft as Taffeta Sarsnet, which felt so, because he never washt his hands, only rub'd his fingers ends slightly with the wet-end of a Napkin, his legs were very weak, having as was thought some foul play in his youth, or rather before he was born, that he was not able to stand at seven years of age, that weakness made him ever leaning on other mens shoulders; his walk was ever circular, his fingers ever in that walk fidling about his cod-piece; he was very intemperate in his drinking.'[5]

These odd habits, which gave rise to much scorn and ribaldry in his lifetime, may have had a simple explanation. John Little, a nineteenth-century physician at the London Hospital, suggested to the Obstetrical Society that James' eccentric behaviour was consistent with the symptoms of what is now known as cerebral palsy, a diagnosis which seems more persuasive than many medical excursions into the health of historical characters.[6] Without the benefit of this diagnosis his contemporaries put the worst possible interpretations on his behaviour.

Whatever his state of health, James' character cannot fail to have been influenced by the appalling circumstances of his upbringing. When his mother, Mary Queen of Scots, was six months' pregnant with him, her secretary, David Rizzio (who was suspected of being the boy's father), was torn from her arms in her bedchamber by a gang of men led by her husband, the violent Henry Stuart, Lord Darnley and butchered outside her door. Before James was a year old Darnley was blown up in his brother's house at Kirk o' Field (and possibly strangled for good measure). Mary was kidnapped and allegedly raped by his murderer, James Hepburn, fourth Earl of Bothwell, who forced her to marry him. She was later compelled

---

[5] Sir Anthony Weldon (attrib.), *The Court and Character of King James I*, 1650). See 'Principal sources' below.
[6] See also the Sir Gordon Gordon-Taylor lecture delivered on 23 October 2008.

The Empty Stage

to abdicate by her discontented subjects and James never saw his mother again.

During the young King's childhood, Scotland was ruled by four Regents. The first was shot when he was three; the second killed in a skirmish when he was four; the third died, believed poisoned, when he was five; the fourth lasted several years until he in turn was deposed and executed. In 1582 James, then sixteen, was kidnapped by John Ruthven, third Earl of Gowrie and his supporters and held for eleven months against his will. He was barely twenty when his mother was beheaded by Queen Elizabeth. 'I was', he later wrote, 'alone, without fader or moder, brother or sister, King of this realme, and heir [apparent] of England. This my nakedness made me to be weak and my enemies stark [strong]'.[7]

Despite his odd appearance and mannerisms, James was no fool. As a child he had been well tutored. He was 'learned beyond his years', being proficient in Latin and fluent in several modern languages. As a man he was to acquire a well-stocked library and wrote widely on such subjects as kingship (*Basilikon Doron*), witchcraft (*Daemonologie*), religion (*Meditations on the Lord's Prayer*), even the evils of the weed (*A Counterblaste to Tobacco*). Throughout his life he was a generous patron of the arts. Almost immediately after reaching London he put Shakespeare's acting troupe, the Chamberlain's Men, on the royal payroll, re-naming them the King's Men. He wrote poetry and encouraged a new flowering of that art, and he set up a committee which produced the finest English language translation of the Bible.[8] In the political sphere James brought to an end the ill feeling between England and Spain and did much to promote international trade. He invented the

---

[7] *Memoirs of the Court of King James the First* (London, Lucy Aiken, 1823).
[8] It was far from an entirely original translation, having drawn heavily on the Bishop's Bible and the Great Bible before that.

idea of Great Britain, but failed in his ambition to unite Scotland and England, which to this day remain separate countries ruled by one Sovereign. Perhaps his greatest achievement was to keep his lands peacefully insulated from foreign wars.

But there was a canker at the heart of James' court. As a result, perhaps, of having lived for so long under two of their most powerful monarchs, the English had become addicted to the repellent cult of sycophancy. Obsequious flattery can unsettle even the strongest character, but it fostered in the susceptible James an extravagant view of the importance of the Crown he wore. In his home country he had been accustomed to ruling without a Parliament and when his French cousin (and possible lover) Esmé Stuart put the theory of divine rule into his head it found ready acceptance. 'The state of Monarchy', James told the English Parliament in 1609, 'is the supremest thing upon earth: for Kings are not only God's lieutenants, and sit upon God's throne, but even by God himself they are called Gods'. Little wonder that James felt justified, whenever Parliament became unduly disobliging, to attempt to do without it.

Though long mocked for his personal habits and for his infatuation with Favourites, modern opinion has tended to be kind towards James, one authority even describing him as 'a remarkable man, with a high theoretic sense of his kingship, yet also an adept practical politician, casual, friendly, intellectual, and scholarly'.[9] The more traditional view was expressed by an American scholar:

> 'Deceived by an exaggerated opinion of his own learning, which was not inconsiderable, and of his capacity for government, which was very small, and confirmed in this delusion by the disgraceful flattery of his courtiers and bishops, James faced real difficulties. He was a foreigner, only rather distantly connected with the Eng-

---

[9] Jenny Wormald, 'James VI and I (1566–1625)', in *Oxford Dictionary of National Biography* (Oxford, Oxford University Press, 2004).

lish royal line, and had come from a hostile and hateful Kingdom to succeed the most renowned of sovereigns and to grasp a scepter that deep policy and long experience had taught her admirably to handle.'[10]

The truth probably lies somewhere between these two extremes.

THE GROOM OF THE BEDCHAMBER

One of the Scottish courtiers James brought with him to London was Robert Carr, his surname now Anglicized to blend into his new environment. There was little he could do about his strong Caledonian accent, but that was no impediment in the court of the Scottish King. (Even in his later years James could not throw off his sometimes impenetrable Scottish burr.) At this period Carr was a beardless young man of slightly androgynous appearance who was described as 'of a bold disposition, comely visage and proportionable personage, mixed with a courtly presence'.[11] It did not take long for James to be taken with the nineteen-year-old youth, whom he appointed a groom of the bedchamber, one of a group of young men who enjoyed intimate access to their monarch.

Over time James' feelings towards the young man turned from fascination to infatuation, but it was not until years later that their relationship became widely known, and it happened in a very public way.

---

[10] Joseph Allen Matter, *My Lords and Lady of Essex: Their State Trials* (Chicago, Henry Regnery Company, 1969), p. 91.
[11] Michael Sparke, *The Narrative History of King James for the First Fourteen Years* (London, 1651).

THE TILTING YARD

When a pageant was held in Whitehall to mark the fourth anniversary of James' accession to the throne, Robert was rewarded with the role of a shield bearer, but things did not go as expected. As he rode towards the King, Robert's horse suddenly reared, throwing its rider to the ground and breaking his leg. James, visibly agitated, called for his personal physician, Theodore de Mayerne to attend the lad. After this, the King became a constant visitor to Robert's chamber for the purpose, it was put about, of teaching him Latin. For James, there was nothing new in an obsession with a handsome young man. The most recent of these had been Philip Herbert whom he had elevated to the rank of earl.[12] When Philip learned of the King's new obsession he is said to have shrugged, cursed and returned to his beloved horses.

Carr's contemporary, the clergyman and poet, Nicholas Oldisworth, had the measure of the new man:

> 'His handsome face and stately figure were embellished by the natural grace of his movements. He understood the niceties of ruffs and frills. He showed an equal taste in the cut of his doublet and in the colour of his hose. In brief, he was master of all those qualities which should easily endear him to the wisest fool in Christendom.[13] His deficiencies, cunningly disguised, were as conspicuous as his gifts. He had as little talent for affairs as for scholarship. In any other Court, save that of James, he would have remained a mere gentleman of the household, and done his best to still the voices of ambition and avarice.'[14]

Soon after the episode of the tiltyard, Carr was knighted and appointed a gentleman of the bedchamber, one step up from groom.

---

[12] Philip Herbert, Earl of Montgomery. He was by birth the second son of the Earl of Pembroke.
[13] A title sometimes attributed to Henry of Navarre.
[14] Nicholas Oldisworth, *A booke touching Sir Thomas Overbury* (1637).

The role of this privileged few was to serve the King's personal needs by taking turns sleeping in his room as bodyguard, assisting him to dress and waiting on him when he ate in private. More significantly, the grooms also controlled access to the monarch, a right which brought with it a considerable degree of patronage. It was not long before Carr became the first among his equals, greatly strengthening his hand at court. 'No suit, no petition, no grant, no letter', it was said, 'but Mr Carr must have a hand in it; so that great rewards are bestowed upon him by suitors and large sums of money by His Majesty, by which means his wealth increased with his favour ...'.[15] The following year, James acknowledged his Favourite's services by giving him 'a tablet of gold set with diamonds'; it was only the first of many lavish gifts.

Thomas Howard, Earl of Suffolk was one of the first to realize what was happening. He wrote to his friend, Sir John Harrington, describing how:

> 'Carr hath all the favours ... The King doth much covet his presence: the ladies, too, are not behind hand in their admiration; for, I tell you, good knight, this fellow is straight-limbed, well-favoured, and smooth-faced, with some sort of cunning and show of modesty, though, God wot, he well knoweth when to show his impudence ... We are almost worn out in our endeavours to keep pace with this fellow in his duty and labour to gain favour, but in vain; where it endeth I cannot guess, but honours are talked of speedily for him.'[16]

And so it proved to be. The young man was showered with increasingly valuable gifts from his Sovereign, the most generous of them (in January 1609) being the manor of Sherborne in Dorset. Confiscated from Sir Walter Raleigh upon his conviction for treason, it was worth about £1,000 a year. Raleigh's wife begged on

---

[15] Michael Sparke.
[16] Quoted in G.B. Harrison, *England in Shakespeare's Day*.

Passion, Poison and Power

her knees to retain the property, but James ignored her pleadings, reportedly muttering, 'I mun have it; I mun have it for Carr'. In fact, James took the property back later to give to his son and heir, Prince Henry. Even then, Carr did not lose out, being awarded the vast sum of £20,000 in compensation.

Young Robert's star continued to rise. In March 1611 he was created Viscount Rochester. Two months later he received the Barony of Winwick and was installed as a Knight of the Garter. Later that year he was made Keeper of the Palace of Westminster and granted the castle of Rochester. And in April 1612, though still only twenty-five years of age, he was appointed a member of the English Privy Council. (He was to receive further titles, but with all this confusion of honours the reader might find it simpler if Carr continues to be so called from hereon, except where the context otherwise requires.)

It should not be thought that, as between Carr and his king, the affections were all one way. When in December 1612 James was confined to bed with diarrhoea, Carr displayed unusual kindness in acting as his nurse. And in the following year when the royal coffers were 'at a dead list' he is said to have 'sent for some officers of the Receit and delivering them the keys of a chest, bid them take what they found there for the King's use, which they say was four or five and twenty thousand pounds in gold'.[17] The novelist and journalist, Philip Gibbs suggested that this was effectively a bribe, but this seems unlikely since on another occasion Carr is known to have refused a royal offer of £8,000, stating that 'he had no reason to be so chargeable to him since he was in necessity himself, and would content himself with those means which his Majesty had already bestowed upon him'.[18]

---

[17] Letter from John Chamberlaine to Winwood.
[18] Letter from John Packer to Sir Thomas Edmondes.

In time, James came to look to Carr for advice on matters of state, using him as a sort of unofficial secretary. But it was not a task for which he was well fitted; administration, which involved writing in the flowery language of the day, was not Carr's strongest suit. Fortunately for him, help was at hand in the form of his old friend, Overbury, who had also followed the new King to London.

THE RISE OF OVERBURY

Overbury had exactly the talents which the younger man lacked and the Privy Councillor gradually began using him to read and comment on State papers, even to the extent of drafting documents which he could present to the King as his own. Carr's dependence on his confidential secretary became so strong that Overbury was sometimes called 'Carr's wit'. It was said that Carr 'could enter into no scheme, nor pursue any measure without the advice and concurrence of Overbury nor could Overbury enjoy any felicity but in the company of him he loved; their friendship was the subject of court conversation, and their genius seemed so much alike, that it was reasonable to suppose no breach could ever be produced between them'.[19]

As Carr advanced in favour so Overbury rose along with him. The Domestic State Papers for 1607, for example, contain an entry recording that, 'The bill concerning Sir Thos. Overbury is signed, through the importunity of Sir Robert Carr'. The older man's first official appointment, obtained for him by his patron, was as sewer (or server) at the King's table. Overbury took full advantage of his office by noting down the conversations which he overheard. (They were to be published long after his death under the title, *Crumbs Fallen from King James' Table*.) In the same year, in recognition

---

[19] Theophilus Cibber, *Lives of the Poets*, Vol. 2, p. 30.

of his place in Carr's affections, property rights in Worcestershire were conferred upon Overbury by a grateful King. In 1608 he was knighted at Carr's request, a mere six months after his patron had been so honoured. At the same time his barrister father was made a judge of the Welsh Marches.

For reasons which are by no means clear, Overbury left for France and the Low Countries the following year. A contemporary record refers to him as being, 'hindered of his expectations by some of his enemies'. Some suggest that he had somehow offended the Queen. Whatever the cause, he took advantage of the opportunity and 'furnish[ed] ... himself with things fitting a statesman, by experience in foreign government, knowledge of the language, passages of employment, external courtship, and good behaviour – things not common to every man'.[20] (He published a record of his experience in his *Observations in his Travels upon the state of the 17 Provinces as they stood anno Dom. 1609.*) Six months later, Overbury returned to London where his rise continued as if it had never been interrupted.

Overbury's unofficial position as right hand man to the King's Favourite was described as bringing with it 'the good affection and favour not only of Sir Robert [Cecil], but of others also. In process of time, this favour procures profit, profit treasure, treasure honour, honour larger employments, and, in time, better execution'.[21] It was said that even the great Sir Francis Bacon had to 'stoop and crouch to Sir Thomas in hope of Somerset's favour to be Master of the Court of Wards; for which place he offered much, and Sir Thomas's father might once have had £1,000 if he would have spoken effectually to his son'.[22] This degree of patronage on the

---

[20] *The Harleian Miscellany* (London, 1810).
[21] *The Harleian Miscellany, ibid.*
[22] Arthur Wilson, *History of Great Britain, Being the Life and Reign of King James I* (1653), p. 56.

part of someone with no official standing at court bred resentment: even James was put out when he got to hear of the popular saying that, 'while Carr rules the King, Overbury rules Carr'. What sort of a man was this who wielded such influence at the heart of the court?

Overbury had a capable, though not brilliant, mind. He was widely read and of a distinct literary bent after having mixed so much in literary circles in his early days at the Temple. Even the poet and playwright, Ben Jonson was sufficiently impressed to pen an effusive epigram to him. ('O Phœbus make me worthy of his Bays,/As but to speak thee, Overbury, is praise').[23] As with so many of Overbury's friendships, however, this one ended in tears, reportedly because the upright Jonson refused to act as a go-between with the unhappily married Lady Rutland. In any event, these literary acquaintances seem to have contributed to the renown which Overbury was to acquire after his death. But it was a bubble reputation, based almost entirely on a single poem.

Although circulated privately in manuscript during his lifetime, *A Wife*[24] was only published posthumously, but it was an immediate success, resulting in a second edition bearing the extended title, *A wife now the widdow of Sir Thomas Overburye ... whereunto are added many witty characters ... written by himselfe and other learned gentlemen his friends.* The book's fame rests largely on these 'characters' – pen portraits of imaginary persons, which have been assumed by reason of the title to be the work of other more distinguished writers. However, John Considine argues

---

[23] Epigram CXIII (1610).
[24] The poem, which is also known as *The Wife*, is said to be the origin of the term, 'skin deep' in referring to beauty. The context is: '... all the carnall beauty of my wife, Is but skin deep'. Ben Jonson claimed that it was written in order to further his attempt to seduce the Countess of Rutland; others had different theories. In fact, it was probably just a poem.

convincingly that 'none of the "Characters" ... were written by Overbury, nor is there any evidence to suggest that any of them were written by anyone associated with him'.[25]

Unfortunately, such merits as Overbury did possess were offset by serious character defects, notably pride, and, which often goes with it, a highly developed talent to give offence. Oldisworth observed that 'not a few men and women at Court were scarred by his mordant tongue'. The historian, Weldon, described him as 'a man of excellent parts, but those made him proud, over-valuing-himself, and under-valuing others, and was infected with a kind of insolency'. The diarist, John Aubrey put it more pithily: 'Sir Thomas Overbury was prouder than Sir Walter Raleigh, who was damnably proud'.[26] It was a defect which was to cost him many friends, possibly his life. As Carr was to remark after Overbury's death, 'I think he had never a friend in his life that he would not sometimes fall out with and give offence unto'.

There are a few slight hints of a sexual element in Overbury's friendship with Carr. The King's Master of Requests, Sir Roger Wilbraham, for example, disparagingly referred to Overbury as Carr's 'bedfellow, minion and inward counsellor'. Many years later, Bacon characterized the pair more obliquely as having had 'an ... excess of friendship'. A strong bond undoubtedly existed between the two men for many years and it is understandable that some should interpret its bitter ending as a lover's quarrel. In fact, there is no evidence whatever to support such a conclusion and the rumours probably derive from nothing more than envy or spite. The same cannot be said of Carr's relations with the King.

---

[25] John Considine, 'The invention of the literary circle of Sir Thomas Overbury', in Claude J. Summers and Ted-Larry Pebworth, *Literary circles and cultural communities in Renaissance England* (Columbia, University of Missouri Press, 2000).
[26] John Aubrey, *Brief Lives*.

Carr's remorseless rise at court places him firmly in a long but not always distinguished line of Favourites, men showered with wealth and titles by a doting sovereign. No one was put out when a King took a royal mistress, but if the object of his affection was a man it was assumed, usually with justification, that the association was of an illicit nature, such as had notoriously been the case between Edward II and Piers Gaveston. This assumption has caused many to ask, what precisely was the relationship between James and his Favourites?

THE ROLE OF THE FAVOURITE

Much ink has been spilled concerning the nature of James' sexuality; and little wonder. At the age of thirteen this affection-starved lad formed a crush for his second cousin, the thirty-seven-year-old Esmé Stuart, Sieur d'Aubigny. In the words of the Scots chronicler Moysie, 'he conceived an inward affection to the Lord d'Aubigne, and entered in great familiarity and quiet purposes with him'. James raised Stuart to the peerage as the Earl of March and lavished a string of favours on him. This rapid rise to eminence was resented so much by some of the Scottish aristocracy that they were moved to kidnap the young King and hold him captive until he agreed to send the Frenchman back to France; the two men never met again. In the early 1600s Philip Herbert, the sixteen-year-old son of the Earl of Pembroke, was the next to conquer James' heart. His gambling debts were paid off and he was created the first Earl of Montgomery. Herbert in his turn was to be replaced by Carr, although he continued to enjoy the King's friendship.[27]

---

[27] Other Favourites are said to have included Alexander Lindsay, Lord Spynie and Francis Stewart Hepburn, Earl of Bothwell.

A seventeenth-century historian, admittedly no lover of Kings, sneeringly described the:

> 'love [James] showed [his Favourites] as amorously conveyed as if he had mistaken their sex, and thought them ladies. ... Nor was his love, or whatever posterity will please to call it, ... carried on with discretion sufficient to cover a less scandalous behaviour; for the King's kissing them after so lascivious a mode in public ... prompted many to imagine some things done in the tiring room that exceed my expression no less than my experience.'[28]

It was hardly a surprising judgement given the way James behaved in public, but was it correct in what it implied?

There is no question that James was capable of heterosexual relations. In 1589 he had married the beautiful sixteen-year-old Anne of Denmark, by whom he was to have five children. When the marriage cooled he went on to enjoy a two-year affair with Anne Murray, later Lady Glamis. All of James' Favourites were similarly capable of 'normal' heterosexual relations. Esmé Stuart was a married man with children before he met James. At the urging of the King, Philip Herbert married Susan de Vere, daughter of the Earl of Oxford. Carr too was to marry with James' blessing, as was the King's last Favourite, Buckingham. But the fact of these marriages in no way rules out the possibility of James' Favourites having at the same time homosexual relations.

In James' day, as now, the prurient were much vexed by the questions of whether there was a physical dimension to the undoubtedly intimate relations between the King and his Favourites and, if so, what form it took. Attitudes to sexuality in those days were far from liberal. Despite the fact that it was a crime punishable by death, sodomy was probably as widespread as it is today. (The great Francis Bacon, for example, was a homosexual

---

[28] *Some Traditional Memorials on the Reign of King James* in *The Works of Francis Osborne*, 9th edn (London, 1689), p. 476.

with a penchant for young boys. Though widely known, this fact was never publicly acknowledged.) Sodomy had been condemned by James himself in his book, *Basilikon Doron*. He had also had it removed from the list of offences which should be included in a general pardon.[29] The significance of all this, unfortunately, is clouded by the fact that at that date there was no general agreement as to exactly what the term 'sodomy' meant. (The ancient Romans, for example, condemned buggery, but only in respect of the man who assumed the female role.) While there was undoubtedly a homoerotic element in James' relationships with all his Favourites, no one can say for sure what form it took; it may well have varied from one man to another. But in truth the physical nature of the King's sex life mattered little; what was important was the love he bore these men, which was deep, and the effects it had upon them, which in some cases were profound.

But it was not Carr's sexual orientation but other tensions at court which were to pose a threat to the King's Favourite and his friend and adviser, Overbury.

THE MASQUE OF HYMEN

Two of the most powerful families at James' court were those of Suffolk and Essex.

The Howards, or the Earls of Suffolk as they had become in 1603, were one of the most powerful – and ambitious – families in the land. As Catholic sympathizers their fortunes had varied with the times, but under the crypto-Catholic James this was a good time. Thomas Howard, first Earl of Suffolk, had distinguished himself in the wars with Spain (he had commanded *The Golden Lion* in the

---

[29] Jeremy Bentham was to denounce the King as a hypocrite for his attitude on the subject.

attack on the Armada) and deserved his country's favour. More to the point, he had supported James' claim to the English throne. When James VI of Scotland added James I of England to his many titles, he rewarded his 'honest big Suffolk' with the appointment of Lord Chamberlain, or chief officer of the court.

By contrast, the Devereux family, or the Earls of Essex as they had become in 1572, had fallen badly from grace. Robert Devereux, the third Earl, was Queen Elizabeth's one-time Favourite who had lost his head in a foolish attempt to take control of the Crown. Fortunately for his son, one of Robert's wiser choices had been surreptitiously to lend his support to James' ambition to succeed Elizabeth on the English throne, a debt which was to be repaid after his death when James restored the family titles to his son, also named Robert, and gave him the honour of bearing the royal sword at his coronation.

There had long been ill feeling between the Howards and the Devereux. (Thomas Howard had served on the commission that condemned Robert's father.) Realizing which way the wind was blowing, and with a daughter to marry off, Howard, possibly prompted by Robert Cecil, had no difficulty in persuading James to arrange a reconciliation between the two families. And so it was that Robert Devereux came to marry Frances Howard on 5 January 1606. Neither bride nor groom had had any say in the matter; the betrothal was a purely dynastic act.

Thirteen-year-old Frances was the younger daughter of Thomas Howard and his second wife, Katherine Knyvett. As a child, she was said to have been 'of the best nature and sweetest disposition of all her father's children, exceeding them also in the delicacy and comeliness of her person'. Her marriage to the fourteen-year-old Robert was a grand affair. King James himself gave the bride away, presenting the young couple with bountiful gifts of plate, jewels and money. The elaborate celebrations began with *The Masque of Hymen* performed on their marriage day by the lords and ladies of the court at the Banqueting Hall in Whitehall.[30] The libretto was written by Ben Jonson, and the music by his collaborator, Alfonso Ferrabosco the younger. The costumes and stage set were designed by Inigo Jones, and the choreography by the dancing master, Thomas Giles. It was a stunning spectacle right from the start. Five white clothed pages entered one side of a stage empty except for a Roman altar:

> 'Behind them, one representing a bridegroom: his hair short, and bound with party-colored ribands, and gold twist; his garments purple and white. On the other hand entered HYMEN (the god of marriage) in a saffron-color'd robe, his under vestures white, his socks yellow, a yellow veil of silk on his left arm, his head crowned with roses and marjoram, in his right hand a torch of pine-tree.'

They in turn were followed by 'a personated bride, supported, her hair flowing and loose, sprinkled with gray; on her head a garland of roses, like a turret; her garments white: and on her back a wether's fleece hanging down: her zone or girdle about her waist of white wool, fastened with the Herculean knot'.

Every bit as spectacular as the actors were the stage mechanics, notably a:

> 'sphere of fire, in the top of all, encompassing the Air, and imitated with such art and industry, as the Spectators might discern the Motion (all the time the Shews lasted) without any Mover; and that so swift, as no Eye could distinguish any colour of the light, but might form to itself Five hundred several hews, out of the translucent body of the Air, objected betwixt it, and them.'

The wedding was followed by nearly a week of festivities. The event could not seemingly have been more propitious, yet it proved to be merely the opening act of a tragedy of truly Jacobean proportions.

---

[30] Not the present Banqueting House designed by Inigo Jones, but its predecessor.

Although such youthful marriages were not unusual (the age of consent then being only twelve), consummation was customarily postponed until the couple were older; so, after some eighteen months presumably spent completing his studies at Oxford, Robert was packed off on the Grand Tour, while Frances returned to her family's mansion, the recently built Audley End in Essex. But she was not to be bored; she had all the pleasures of the court to explore. It was a court stamped with the character of its King.

IN THE COURT OF THE SCOTTISH KING

The court which Frances entered at so young an age has often been portrayed as one of financial extravagance and sexual debauchery as expressed in the extravagant and immodest styles of clothing which were then fashionable. The Puritan, Lucy Hutchinson, described the court as 'a nursery of lust and intemperance'. Anne Turner, who lived on the fringes of the court and was to play an important role in our story, was to declare that 'there is no religion in most of (the King's servants), but malice, pride, whoredom, swearing and rejoicing in the fall of others; it is so wicked a place I wonder that the earth did not open and swallow it up'. Another contemporary, Sir Foulke Greville, described how, 'The holy estate of matrimony [was] most perfidiously broken, and, amongst many, made but a May-game; by which means, divers private families have been subverted, brothel-houses in abundance tolerated, and even great persons prostituting their bodies ...'.[31] Even the King, himself a heavy drinker, had acquired a reputation for tolerating drunken, lascivious behaviour.

No doubt, many of the courtiers did lead less than chaste lives, but recent scholarship tends to regard tales of widespread

---

[31] Quoted in *The Harleian Miscellany* (London, 1810). Foulke Greville described himself on his tomb as 'Servant of Queen Elizabeth, Counsellor to King James, Friend to Sir Philip Sidney'.

debauchery as over-egged. One historian, for example, pointed out that the alleged 'corruption' turned mainly on three episodes: the Overbury case and two occasions when court entertainment went badly wrong as a result of drink. 'It hardly amounts', she wrote, to '*the* corrupt court'.[32] Nevertheless, the court of King James was probably not somewhere a concerned mother would wish to see her daughter.

Unfortunately, Frances' mother was a lady of indifferent morals quite unfitted to act as a chaperone, particularly for someone so young and attractive as her daughter. It was a situation which was bound to lead to trouble.

---

[32] Jenny Wormald, 'James VI and I (1566–1625)', in *Oxford Dictionary of National Biography* (Oxford, Oxford University Press, 2004).

ACT 2

THE HUSBAND, HIS WIFE AND HER LOVERS

Essex returned to England in Christmas 1609 after a slightly less than Grand Tour of France and the Low Countries; he was nearly eighteen and determined to claim his bride, now renowned as one of the most beautiful women at court. But Essex the young groom had grown into a proud, hot-tempered man whose interests – in war and field sports – were so very different from those of the stylish society beauty his wife had become. When the couple were reunited as husband and wife she did not like his way of life and she did not like him.

And proximity did not breed affection, particularly when Essex removed his wife from court to the bucolic pleasures of his summer retreat at Chartley in Staffordshire. Arthur Wilson records her reaction:

> '... she shut herself up in her Chamber, not suffering a Beam of light to peep upon her dark Thoughts. If she stirr'd out of her Chamber; it was in the dead of Night, when sleep had taken possession of all others but those about her. In this implacable and discontented Humour she continu'd some Months, always murmuring against, but never giving the least civil Respect to her Husband ...'

As time passed without any signs of pregnancy tongues began to wag; and not without reason. Though sharing a bed, the young couple were not enjoying the normal pleasures of newlyweds.

Robert complained to Frances' parents about her lack of interest in the physical side of their marriage and they took his part in the quarrel; but it was not an area in which a young woman could be coerced and the stand-off continued. It was not long before Frances left Robert to stay with her parents at Audley End.

Shortly after his return to England, Robert had suffered a serious bout of smallpox from which he barely survived. It left him with a badly scarred face which his American biographer, Vernon F. Snow, has suggested might have caused him to withdraw from social gatherings, ceremonials and even the court, a disposition which only served to estrange his wife still further.[1] He in turn complained that she had become 'farded and sophisticated' by the dissolute court life.[2] This may have been true, but the young couple's real problem was their incompatibility. What had begun as a simple lack of affection on Frances' part soon turned to violent dislike of her 'grumbling Essex'. It was not as if she lacked other young men only too willing to take his place.

During her husband's twenty-one months' absence abroad, Frances' name had been linked at various time with those of a number of promising young courtiers, even the heir to the throne. Henry Frederick Stuart, Prince of Wales and once Essex's boon companion, was a popular young man. It was said that 'both for wisdom and strength of body there was not such another to be found amongst the English'.[3] Contemporary observers noted the ways in which Henry was attracted by Frances and laid court to her. The seventeenth-century antiquarian, Sir Simonds D'Ewes saw a guiding hand behind the relationship when he described how

---

[1] Vernon F. Snow, *Essex the Rebel* (Lincoln, University of Nebraska Press, 1970).
[2] Arthur Wilson, *The History of Great Britain, Being the Life and Reign of King James I* (1653). 'Farded' meant someone who painted her face.
[3] Michael Sparke.

Frances, 'being set on by the Earl of Northampton, her father's uncle, first caught his eye and heart, and afterwards prostituted herself to him, who first reaped the fruits of her virginity'.[4]

There can be no certainty that the Prince actually did enjoy Frances' more intimate pleasures (the suggestion did not emerge until much later), but it was not long before her eyes turned towards another. Once again, the hand which seems to have hovered like a shadow over the relationship was that of her great uncle, Henry Howard, first Earl of Northampton.

NORTHAMPTON

Northampton was a talented and complex character. There was no doubt about his intelligence: he had acquired a Master's degree in classics from Cambridge and a Master's in civil law from Oxford before returning to Cambridge to become Reader in rhetoric. Bishop Godwin described him as 'the learnedest man among the nobility and the most noble among the learned'.[5] He was always in need of money to further his love of building and patronage of the arts, a patronage which was to leave him at his death with heavy debts. As a closet Catholic who received a secret pension from Spain, he was to be arrested and imprisoned five times. A man of dangerous ambitions, John Nichols judged him to be 'a pedant dark and mysterious'.[6] Sir Francis Bacon's mother probably had his measure when she described him as, 'a dangerous, intelligenc-

---

[4] Not everyone took so cynical a view of Frances' relations with the Prince, notably Sir Charles Cornwallis, the Prince's treasurer. (Thomas Birch, *The Life of Henry, Prince of Wales* (London, A. Miller, 1760)).
[5] Quoted in Andrew Amos, *The Great Oyer of Poisoning: The Trial of the Earl of Somerset for the possible poisoning of Sir Thomas Overbury* (London, Richard Bentley, 1846).
[6] *The Progress, Processions and Magnificent Festivities of King James I*, (London, J B Nichols, 1828).

ing man; no doubt a subtle Papist inwardly, and lieth in wait'. Like his nephew Suffolk, Northampton had supported James' claims to the English throne and had triumphantly accompanied him south to claim it. For this he was rewarded in the fullness of time with the posts of Secretary of State and Lord Privy Seal.[7] At first, he had attached his star to Robert Cecil, but when Carr began to make a name for himself at court, Northampton was prepared to use all his resources to gain the young man's favour. Among these resources were the charms of his great niece, Frances, whom he seems to have had no compunction in propelling in a direction which best served his interests.

Frances' approaches towards Carr were not immediately reciprocated. Indeed, Overbury was to remind him later of the uncomplimentary things he had said about her when they first met. But after a while the Earl began to take the initiative in the affair, using Overbury as his cupid. The older man was induced to carry 'letters to and again between the Countess and the viscount; some to Paternoster-Row; some to Hammersmith, and others to other places of meeting, which were appointed between them ...'.[8] Many of the letters were actually written by Overbury, though it is a mystery why he should have been willing to do this in light of his strong dislike of the Howard family in general and of Frances in particular. Perhaps he thought it was an idle romance which would come to nothing? If so, he was very much mistaken.

Some understanding of the dynamics between Frances, Carr and Essex at this time can be seen from a trivial incident which followed the investiture of the Prince of Wales in June 1610. The event was celebrated, inevitably, by a masque, *Tethys' Festival,*

---

[7] The Lord Privy Seal had charge of the King's personal seal. The job was a sinecure, but an important one in terms of royal favour.
[8] *The Harleian Miscellany* (London, 1810).

written specially for the occasion.[9] The story is that after the masque was over, Carr and Frances were walking to a waiting barge when Carr suddenly seized a riband from her head which she playfully tried to get back. Essex appeared on the scene and dismissed Carr curtly: 'The Countess of Essex does not need your escort', to which Frances tartly rejoined, 'The Countess needs no man's escort'.

But even while Carr was enjoying his status as royal Favourite and the object of Frances' affections, a cloud appeared on the horizon which was to bode ill for the young man.

TROUBLE WITH THE QUEEN

Despite the romantic circumstance in which the King's marriage had begun (James had hastened across the sea to save his proxy bride from a suspected shipwreck) the union was far from happy. Queen Anne had been affronted by her husband's blatant affair with Anne Murray, later Lady Glamis, and by his refusal to permit her any say in the upbringing of their child, Henry. She had even tried, unsuccessfully, to seize the boy by force when James left Scotland to assume the English throne. An accommodation was reached only after the Queen put her foot down and refused to join her husband in London, but it did not end the acrimony between the royal couple. Anne found her husband's drinking and his predilection for male Favourites, notably Carr, unacceptable, particularly because they wielded patronage which she had hitherto enjoyed exclusively and because he failed to show her the respect she felt due.

---

[9] It took the form of a vision of an antique Britain with Tethys representing the Queen of the ocean and Frances as one of her nymphs clad in a diaphanous blue robe on the banks of a river.

The Queen's resentment found expression, as such things often do, in a trivial incident. A contemporary described how in 1611, '[Carr] and his dear Overbury, walking in the garden at Greenwich [palace] whither the Queen's window openeth, she broke into a sudden and contemptible laughing at them. "So", saith she, "they did at her", which belief carried her so far that she went to the King with tears in her eyes and complained'.[10] Bishop Goodman added colour to the story:

> 'The Queen was looking out of her window into the garden, where Somerset and Overbury were walking; and when the Queen saw them, she said, "There goes Somerset and his governor," and a little after Overbury did laugh. The Queen conceiving that he had overheard her, thought they had laughed at her, whereupon she complained, and Overbury was committed.'[11]

Whatever the truth of the matter, a distressed Anne hysterically demanded that the two men be punished for what she saw as their contemptuous behaviour towards her. James adamantly refused to take any action against his beloved Carr, so the Queen turned to Robert Cecil, now Lord Salisbury, and asked him to persuade the Council to punish Overbury (who held no such place in her husband's affections). The result was that the knight was banned from court, a punishment which was only lifted five months later. His return to court, however, was made conditional upon the fact that he should be 'neither in the Queen's sight, nor of her side'.

Thomas Overbury had made his first powerful enemy.

When Frances refused to join her husband, Essex applied to his father in law for custody of his reluctant bride. Suffolk could

---

[10] Downshire MSS, 3.83, quoted in *Oxford Dictionary of National Biography* (Oxford, Oxford University Press, 2004).
[11] Godfrey Goodman, *The Court of James I*. In fact, as will be seen, there was no committal. (The reference to 'Somerset' must be an anachronism since Carr did not acquire this title until two years later.)

Passion, Poison and Power

not refuse and Robert brought her back with him to Chartley. But although the couple were sharing a bed, it did not alter Frances' resolve to have nothing to do with a man she loathed. Essex complained of his wife's 'looseness, of the report of the vulgar, and what a strange course of life she led, contrary to all piety and honesty'. It was a remark which 'stung the Countess to the heart, and more increased and augmented her malice towards him so that in a great fury she takes her coach, and repairs to her ancient acquaintance, Mrs Turner'.[12]

THE GO-BETWEEN AND THE MAGICIAN

Anne Turner was a short, pretty woman in her mid-thirties, the widow of a fashionable physician who lived openly with a friend of her late husband's, by whom she had borne four children. He was Sir Arthur Mainwaring, former carver to Prince Henry and a man of some standing.

Anne herself was not without resources, derived partly from a couple of high-class brothels which she owned, but principally from a saffron-based starch she had invented for dyeing collars and ruffs a fashionable yellow colour.[13] Of yeoman stock, Anne later claimed to have been 'ever brought up with the Countess', though others insisted that the two of them had been brought together by Northampton (for whom, it was rumoured, Anne had once acted as a spy). Whatever the truth of the matter, the friendship between the two women was genuine and so close that it became the subject of gossip. Writing many years later, Roger Coke, grandson of the Chief Justice of the same name, described the 'familiarity between [them] as "publicly scandalous"'. Be that as it may, Anne, who

---

[12] *The Harleian Miscellany* (London, 1810).
[13] The starch is mentioned in Shakespeare's *All's Well That Ends Well* and in Ben Jonson's *The Devil is an Ass*.

enjoyed a reputation for advising on affairs of the heart, responded to Frances' plea for help by putting her in touch with a former associate of her late husband who, she claimed, had used magic to help her seduce her present partner, Mainwaring.

ENTER DOCTOR FORMAN

The notorious doctor Forman was an astrologer, apothecary and necromancer (that is, someone who could summon up the dead), all of which activities were then believed to be closely intertwined. He was the author of a popular book on what passed as medicine, and a recent biographer has gone so far as to compare his skills favourably with those of Dr Mayerne, the King's physician.[14] Unlike Mayerne, Forman had long been in bad odour with the authorities, having twice been imprisoned by the College of Physicians for his unauthorized use of astrology and for his lack of learning. (Once, when compelled to take an examination in his craft, he was reported to have given answers which were judged 'absurd & mirth-provoking'.) Eventually, after gaining a doctorate from Jesus College, Cambridge and, thus, a licence to practise medicine, Forman was able to ignore the College of Physicians and rapidly acquired a reputation as a healer of plague victims. More importantly for Frances' purposes, this weird character had a reputation as someone able to provide potions which could quell or stimulate sexual desire. They were exactly what Frances was looking for, the former to cool her husband's ardour and the latter to inflame her lover's.

Some of the letters which the Countess wrote to Anne Turner and Doctor Forman and managed to smuggle out of Chartley have

---

[14] Judith Cook, *Dr Simon Forman; a most notorious physician* (London, Vintage, 2002).

survived. One of Frances' letters to Anne, which was marked 'Burn this letter', reveals the close relationship which had developed between the two women:

> 'Sweet Turner,
>
> I am out of all hope of any good in this world, for my father, my mother and my brother said, I should lie with him [that is, her husband, Essex] ... I would rather die a thousand times over; for beside the sufferings, I shall lose his [Carr's] love if I lie with him ... I am not able to bear the miseries that are coming on me, but I cannot be happy so long as this man [Essex] liveth ... Let him know this ill news; if I can get this done, you shall have as much money as you can demand; this is fair play.
>
> Your sister, Frances Essex.'

In a letter to Forman, whom she addressed as 'Sweet Father', Frances declared that she had:

> '... no cause but to be confident in you, yet I desire to have it as it is yet remaining well; so continue it still if it be possible, and if you can send me some good fortune; alas, I have need of it. Keep the Lord [Carr] still to me, for that I desire, and be careful you name me not to anybody, for we have so many spies that you must use all your wits, and all little enough, for the world is against me, and I do fear all the heavens favor me not, only happy in your love ... My Lord [Essex] is lusty and merry, and drinketh with his men, and useth me as doggedly as ever before, and all the contentment he give me is to abuse me. I think I shall never be happy in this world, because he hinders all my good, and will ever, I think.'

The letter ended with an injunction to Forman to 'give Turner warning of all things, but not the Lord [that is, Essex]. I would not have anything come out for fear of the Lord Treasurer [Northampton]'. It was signed, 'Your assured, affectionate, loving daughter, Frances Essex'.

At her request, Forman provided Frances with 'love-philters', or aphrodisiacs, in the form of jellies which she bribed Carr's servants to serve to their master. At the same time her husband's servants were prevailed upon to rinse his linen in camphor in the hope of achieving the opposite effect. For good measure she was said to have twisted a thorn into the penis of a wax model of him every evening.[15] Even more bizarrely, it was claimed that she wore 'an artifice too immodest to be expressed to hinder penetration'.[16]

While Carr gradually began to return her affections, none of Foreman's potions had the slightest effect on her husband. In one of her letters to Anne she grumbled, 'My lord is as lusty as ever he was, and hath Complained to my brother Howard, that he hath not lain with me nor used me as his wife. This makes me mad, since of all men I loath him as the only obstacle and hinderance (sic), that I shall never enjoy him whom I love'.[17]

Forman died of natural causes on 8 September 1611 (having accurately predicted the date of his own demise).[18] As soon as she learned of his passing, Anne Turner sent her maid, who rejoiced in the name of Toothless Margaret, to the late doctor's' house to recover from his widow all papers connected with her clients. She threatened that if these documents were not produced the house would be searched and money and property seized. The letters were duly handed over except for the two quoted above, which were held back for reasons we can only guess at. Before we leave Dr Forman it is important to remember that there is no suggestion

---

[15] *History of the First Fourteen Years of King James' Reigne* (Somers Tracts).
[16] William Camden, *Annals of King James I*. Camden was a seventeenth-century antiquarian.
[17] Michael Sparke. 'My brother Howard' referred to Frances' brother, Henry Howard.
[18] He is said to have prophesied that he would perish 'ere Thursday night'. He did in fact die the following Thursday while rowing himself across the Thames (Judith Cook, *Dr Simon Forman; a most notorious physician* (London, Vintage, 2002, p. 196).

Passion, Poison and Power

that he was the source of anything more noxious than aphrodisiacs and anaphrodisiacs.

With Forman dead, Frances contacted two other conjurers of doubtful reputation, a Mr Gresham and a Dr Savory, but their services proved to be unnecessary, probably because her love affair with the Earl had already been consummated. Some time in the spring of 1612, on the way to her husband's home in the country, Frances managed to slip away for a clandestine meeting with her lover in a farmer's house where the pair were said to have 'tarried together about an hour and a half at least'. On another occasion they met at night in one of Mrs Turner's 'houses of leisure' in Paternoster Row. The man who arranged these encounters was a former long-time employee of Anne Turner's by the name of Richard Weston, who was to play a significant part in this story.

Not long after this the King was hit by a personal tragedy which some were to link to Overbury's fate: his beloved son, the Prince of Wales, died suddenly and for no obvious reason.

THE DEATH OF THE PRINCE

For some time the young Prince had been suffering bouts of faintness and sickness. One day in the autumn of 1612 after dining with the King he experienced one of these bouts, but this time accompanied by a fever which confined him to bed tormented with thirst. An eighteenth-century historian described how:

> 'That night, during which he rested ill, he was ordered a cooling tisan with broth at the end of his fit. On Monday, October 26, he felt no abatement of the pain in his head; his belly continued costive, and his pulse high; his water crude, thin, and whitish; which

The Husband, His Wife and Her Lovers

induced Dr. Mayerne, his Majesty's chief Physician, to order him a clyster [or enema], which operated very well.'[19]

Later that day the Prince got up and played cards with friends, but he still 'looked ill and pale, spoke hollow, and strangely, with dead sunk eyes, his dryness of mouth and great thirst continuing ...'. Doctors Naismith and Mayerne were called and wanted to bleed the patient, but soon realized that he was too ill for that. Purges were tried a few days later, but to no effect; the high fever and headache continued. Finally, on the eighth day the doctors resolved that the royal patient must be bled whatever the risk. Yet another doctor was called, but despite all their efforts Henry's decline continued. When he became delirious it was decided to cup his scalp, an uncomfortable procedure which involved shaving parts of his head and placing on them glass cups which had been evacuated of air.

It did no good and in the desperation which comes when all other measures have failed, the doctors turned to folk magic, applying a cloven chicken to the soles of their patient's feet; but again without effect. Realizing that the Prince did not have long to live, he was given the opiate, diascordium, to relieve his pains and the Archbishop was called to prepare him for eternity. Nothing more could be done and at eight o'clock on 6 November the eighteen-year-old Prince finally expired. The court was dismayed at the sudden and unexplained death of one so young and apparently healthy, and his distraught mother was heard to shout out that her son had been poisoned by Sir Thomas Overbury, the man she most despised and distrusted.

But the Queen was no longer his most dangerous enemy.

---

[19] Thomas Birch, *The Life of Henry, Prince of Wales* (London, A. Miller, 1760).

OVERBURY THE STATESMAN

Salisbury had died in May of that year after a long illness, creating a power vacuum at the heart of the court. Competition for the position of Secretary, or first minister to the King, had begun long before his death. At Overbury's initiative, Carr and the Howards agreed to put up joint candidates in the persons of the Protestant, Sir Henry Neville and the ambitious and abrasive Sir Ralph Winwood. According to Viscount Fenton:

> 'Overberrye drew to him and about my Lord of Rotchester are lyke to make a pairtye to [i.e. opposed to] the Howards ... Southehamptoun and Pembrouke are joyned in that syde, and thaye stand mutche to have Nevell Secreterrye. Thaye have vith them sume of the moste discontented nobill men of the younger sort, and all the Parlement mutineers.'

It was the first intimation of Oversbury's dislike of the Howard clan. In the end, the King decided that he could do perfectly well without a Secretary. Northampton assumed much of the burden of government, but it was Carr to whom the King entrusted the signet ring with which royal documents were authenticated.

The responsibilities of his role as acting Secretary strained the twenty-five-year-old Viscount to his limits, but at least he had the sense to realize it and began to lean ever more heavily on Overbury. Bacon later described how 'packets were sent, sometimes opened by my lord, sometimes unbroken, unto Overbury, who perused them, registered them, made table-talk of them, as they thought good: so the time was, when Overbury knew more of the secrets of state than the Council table did'. Overbury, who was already loathed by the Howards for his opposition to Frances' marriage and resented by the Queen for her own reasons, was now disliked even more widely for what was regarded as his meddling in affairs of state. Northampton in particular was heard to mutter darkly 'the scab's mouth must be shut or evil will come of it'. (He and his circle used the word, 'scab' to refer to Overbury.) He warned Carr,

'Unless you either curb his greatness or abate his pride he will in time be your equal in power and greatness'.

But Overbury was not the only issue which divided the court: a far more serious issue was the country's relations with Catholic Spain. Some, such as James and his Catholic-leaning courtiers like the Howards, were in favour of conciliation with England's historic rival.[20] Others, like Overbury, would have preferred an alliance with Protestant Holland. An equally contentious issue was how to get money out of a Parliament well aware that 'supply', as it was called, was its only bargaining counter with the King. In 1611, after it had refused to make the financial provision he had demanded, James, accustomed to personal rule in his native Scotland, finally snapped and dissolved Parliament. Some, such as Salisbury, argued for an accommodation ('the great contract') under which Parliament would be recalled in exchange for financial subventions. Others, like the Howards, supported the King's more confrontational attitude. Three years later, James was forced to restore Parliament, but dissolved it yet again after only eight weeks sitting, after the Commons complained about the impositions (excise duties) which had been imposed on the people.[21] A jubilant Northampton paraded around London with forty followers. It was to be his last triumph, for he died a week later.

Long before Northampton's death, but against the background of political unrest and personal unhappiness which preceded it, a desperate Frances had turned for help to yet another magical source.

---

[20]   James may have been influenced by the pension he was secretly receiving from that country for services rendered.
[21]   Parliament had no time to pass any bills and for this reason was known as the 'addled' Parliament.

'CUNNING MARY'

Mary Woods, or 'Cunning Mary' as she was known,[22] was a practitioner in rural magic who had left her Norfolk village for London in order to make her fortune. She established herself in premises in The Strand from which she ran a fashionably successful practice in charms and medicines. Her involvement with the Countess only came to light after she decamped with a ring which she had been given. Frances' servant, Grimstone, was sent to get it back. When he caught up with Mary she claimed that she had sold the ring and threatened that if she was exposed she would tell the authorities that her mistress had given her money and jewels in order to poison the Earl, her husband. The Countess, she claimed, had asked her for 'a kind of poison that would lie in a man's body three or four days without swelling'. Undeterred, Grimstone complained to a local justice of the peace, saying, somewhat unconvincingly, that the ring had been given to Mary for convenience while Frances went to court.

Mary was arrested and taken to London for examination. By then her story had changed: she had, she said, been given the ring in part payment for a powder which she had provided for Lady Essex to wear round her neck in order to conceive a child. Legal proceedings were begun, but dropped in unexplained circumstances. It may be, as some have suggested, that Mary was no more than a thief who had been caught out; if so, she seems to have been remarkably familiar with Frances' innermost desires. We will never know.

Whether by magic or by inclination, Carr was now well and truly smitten with Frances and the couple began to proclaim their love by wearing 'yellow bands, dusted haire, curled, crisped, frisled,

---

[22] 'Cunning' simply meant skilful.

The Husband, His Wife and Her Lovers

slicked skins, opened breasts beyond accustomed modesty'.[23] It was hardly surprising that the Earl began to let his court work slide. His neglect proved to be his friend's opportunity:

> 'insomuch that all must lie upon Overbury's neck; and this doth he honestly, and to the viscount's credit, attributing every action to his doing, although of him neglected: answers for him, in his absence, hastens dispatches in his presence; furthers the requests of suitors, and, through the neglect and carelessness of the viscount, grows in greater credit and esteem, so that his carefulness, sufficiency, and diligence, make him become eminent, and beloved both of the King and council.'[24]

But, like the butterfly with the flame, Overbury was to discover that there are dangers in getting too close to the light.

---

[23] Michael Sparke.
[24] *The Harleian Miscellany* (London, 1810).

ACT 3

THE ANNULMENT

Robert and Frances are thought to have shared a bed together for the last time shortly after Christmas 1612. Accounts differ as to exactly what took place that night at a relative's house in The Strand, but whatever it was it certainly did not involve either sex or affection.

By this stage the Howard family had reluctantly come to accept that Frances was not going to produce an heir with her husband and that the best thing would be for her to be lawfully united with her lover. It was a dramatic *volte face,* but there remained the tricky question of how such a union could be brought about at a time when divorce was virtually unobtainable. Fortunately for the reluctant bride, there was then, as there is now, an alternative to divorce available in certain circumstances, namely annulment of marriage.

Annulment had begun in the thirteenth century as an ecclesiastical remedy. One of the grounds upon which it was available was that the marriage had not been consummated for three years while the couple had been sleeping together. But there was a problem with this: few men, even today, are willing to admit that they are impotent. In the time of the dynastic obsessed Jacobeans it was the kiss of death. Essex was particularly sensitive on this point; indeed, when a member of the Howard family made

The Annulment

some contemptuous remark along these lines he challenged him to a duel, though it came to nothing.

The dilemma was finally resolved at a round table conference between the Howard and the Essex families. To everyone's relief, Robert agreed to an ingenious plan devised by Henry Wriothesley, Earl of Southampton and his friend William Herbert, Earl of Pembroke, whereby he would not object to the proposed annulment so long as it was understood that his inability between the sheets was confined solely to his wife. It was an elegant solution. It fell short of stigmatizing Essex as impotent towards womankind in general, thus preserving his virility. And if he was subsequently discovered to have had sex with a woman it would not lay him open to a charge of perjury. (The agreement was of course an attempt to pervert the course of justice, but this does not seem to have bothered anyone involved.)

Although we do not know what passed between the King and the Howards, James, who was as anxious as everyone else to see an end to the strained relations between the two families, moved swiftly to appoint an ecclesiastical Commission to hear Frances' application for annulment of marriage.

OVERBURY'S REACTION

No one knows the circumstances in which Overbury got to hear of the plan for ending Frances' marriage and marrying Carr, but when he came to realize its full implications they must have hit him hard. If his patron were to become a member of the Howard clan he so much despised they would, he must have feared, soon replace himself in his friend's affections, his only source of power and influence. It was not something he was prepared to tolerate. Where others might have trodden carefully, Overbury chose the path of confrontation. He told his patron bluntly that his lover and intended wife, Frances, was a strumpet and her parents, bawds. He warned that 'marrying the Countess would not only be hurtful to his preferment, but helpful to subvert and overthrow him'. 'Who would' he asked, '(being possessed of so great possibilities as he was, so great honours and large revenues, and daily in expectation of others) cast all away upon a woman, noted for her injury and immodesty, and pull upon himself the hatred and contempt of great personages for so small a matter?'.[1]

Carr did not react well to this advice and stormy scenes ensued. Matters came to a head when, returning to his chambers late one night, he chanced upon Overbury in 'the privy-gallery at Whitehall'. According to Henry Payton, his master, Overbury asked Carr, 'What do you here at this time of night?'. When he got no reply he went on bitterly, 'Will you never leave the company of that base woman? And seeing you do so neglect my advice, I desire that tomorrow morning we may part and that you will let me have that portion you know is due to me; and then I will leave you free to yourself, to stand on your own legs'. Carr retorted that his legs were strong enough to bear himself; and so departed in great displeasure. The break could not have been more final.

But if Carr was offended by Overbury, Frances was furious with him, both for his unrestrained abuse of herself and her family and for his interference with her marital plans. As someone privy to her affair with Carr – and possibly other men – Overbury was in a position to destroy Frances' hopes of an annulment, which depended of course upon her status as a virgin. She is said to have reacted by '[mustering] up all her passions with the greatest

---

[1] 'Introduction', in Edward F. Rimbault, Ll.D. (ed.), *The Miscellaneous Works in Prose and Verse of Sir Thomas Overbury Knt., Now First Collected* (London, John Russell Smith, 1856). *The Harleian Miscellany* (London, 1810) suggested that Overbury's poem, *The Wife* was written in order to warn Carr off his proposed marriage to Frances, but this is not obvious from the text.

acrimony that a feminine malice could devise, [and] never left till she had discharged all the volleys of her rage upon him'.[2] But rage was not enough for the Countess: as she told her friend Anne Turner, 'I cannot be happy so long as this man liveth. He must be put out of the way altogether'.

Frances' first plan was to stage a violent quarrel designed to result in Overbury's death. On 13 April 1613 she approached Sir David Wood (or Woodes), one of the Queen's Scottish servants who was known to bear a grievance against Sir Thomas, to inquire whether he would be willing to do away with the troublesome knight through the artifice of a staged duel. In return she offered a bribe of £1,000 and a promise to make 'his greatest enemy' – presumably Carr – become his friend. But Wood was 'loath to be carried to Tyburn for the lady's pleasure', and demanded a written promise from Carr to secure the King's pardon. The undertaking was not forthcoming, and this particular plan went nowhere.[3] An alternative strategy was needed.

But bigger beasts than Frances were now eyeing Overbury with apprehension. The Howards, Thomas and Henry, were concerned that if he succeeded in stopping the projected annulment and re-marriage, their family's influence at court would be seriously damaged. Someone, probably Northampton, came up with a plan designed to get Overbury out of the way during the critical annulment proceedings: he would be tempted out of the country with the offer of an embassy abroad.

---

[2] Arthur Wilson, History of Great Britain, 1653.
[3] We have no way of knowing whether Carr refused to provide the guarantee or whether Frances was reluctant to seek his agreement to it.

THE EMBASSY PLOT

The scheme required the King's agreement, which seems to have been readily obtained. George Abbot, Archbishop of Canterbury was despatched from court to make Overbury an informal offer of an embassy, almost certainly Moscow.[4] He turned it down flat. Dismayed at this reaction, James sent a second, more powerful delegation consisting of Lord Ellesmere, the Lord Chancellor, and Pembroke. They assured him that the foreign post was intended as a step toward something greater – Amsterdam and Paris were mentioned – but he would have none of it, offering as his excuse that he had no mastery of any foreign language. When the delegation replied that he was young enough to learn one, he responded by pleading ill health, claiming that he was 'exceedingly troubled by the spleen'. A change of air, the delegation countered, would be good for his health.

Now running out of excuses, Overbury revealed his true colours by turning down the offer in 'undecent [sic] and unmannerly speeches'. When the delegation reported his reaction to the King, they emphasised that the refusal had been 'pregnant with contempt'. (He later tried to excuse his language 'as being surprised on the sudden, and spoken in regard of my sickness, and not of [the King's] command'.) James was infuriated: a royal offer was not something which could be refused without good reason, and none had been offered.

At the King's instructions the Privy Council had Overbury arrested that very day and committed to the Tower of London. In the words of the warrant for his arrest, 'his Matie [Majesty] hath conceaved a greate displeasure against [him] for a matter of high contempt'. Overbury protested that 'the King could not in law nor justice force him to forsake his country'. It was an interesting

---

[4] The question of which embassy Overbury was offered is carefully examined in Chester Dunning, 'The Fall of Sir Thomas Overbury and the Embassy to Russia in 1613', *Sixteenth Century Journal*, Vol. XXII, No. 4, 1991).

The Annulment

objection, but even if he had been made aware of it, James was not in a state to be diverted by such a legal nicety.

Why, then, did Overbury refuse an appointment which would have meant an increase in status for someone like him who had no formal standing at court?

The truth only came out much later from Overbury's servant, Payton. He revealed how an MP, Sir Dudley Digges had been sent by the King to discover Overbury's intentions in the matter of the embassy. He 'found him to rely upon the lord of Somerset, saying. "My precious chief [that is, Carr] knows the King's mind better than any, and I the mind of my precious chief."'. What seems to have happened is that, before giving his answer to the delegation, Overbury had consulted his 'friend' Carr, who assured him that if he refused Moscow another, more attractive, appointment would be made.[5] 'For, saith he, your preferments and your expectations lie not among foreign nations; you are now in credit at home, and have already made trial of the dangers of travel; why then should you hazard all upon uncertainties, being in possession, as a man may say, of all that you may expect by this means already?' It was an ingenious argument which played well on Overbury's pride and ambition, but it was not the end of the Earl's duplicity. In order to be certain of the desired reaction at court, Carr had taken the precaution of going to the King personally to complain of Overbury's insolence, hinting that it was because he felt the office of ambassador to be below him.

None of this was known at the time. Court gossip even speculated that Overbury's committal to the Tower had reflected badly on Carr. So concerned was James that he felt it necessary to assure his Council that he 'meant [Carr] daily more grace and favour, as should be seen in short time; and that he took more delight and contentment in his company and conversation than in any man's living'.[6]

---

[5] *The Harleian Miscellany* (London, 1810).
[6] Letter from Chamberlaine to Winwood dated 6 May 1613, in *Memorials*.

Overbury entered the Tower of London on 21 April 1613 and never left that frightful place.[7] What happened to him while he was there is a question which is hotly debated to this day.

---

[7] There is a tradition that he was, like the Somersets, lodged in the Bloody Tower (William Hepworth Dixon, *His Majesty's Tower* (1870), Arthur T. Poyser, *The Tower of London* (1808), George John Younghusband, *A short history of the Tower of London* (1926), and the Historic Royal Palaces website).

ACT 4

OVERBURY IN THE TOWER

Once Overbury was securely lodged in the Tower, Northampton acted swiftly to ensure that he was wholly within his power.

A fortnight or so after he had been committed Carr persuaded the Privy Council to dismiss the upright Lieutenant of the Tower, Sir William Wade (or Waad), on a dubious charge of negligence. His replacement was Sir Gervase Elwes (or Helwyss), Northampton's creature, who had been induced to pay a fee of £2,000 for the privilege (not an unusual practice at the time).[1] Elwes was later to claim that Wade had been dismissed for carelessly allowing another prisoner, the King's cousin Lady Arbella (or Arabella) Stuart, to have a key to her cell, but there can be no doubt that the real reason for his removal was to put Overbury firmly in the plotters' hands.

Northampton had chosen the new Lieutenant carefully. Elwes was, according to Sir Henry Wotton, 'somewhat of an unknown man'. In fact, he was a country gentleman who had gone to Cambridge and trained as a barrister in the Middle Temple. More to the point, he was also a client of Thomas Howard, Frances' father,

---

[1] According to Sir Henry Wotton, both Carr and his wife were instrumental in the appointment.

and an inveterate gambler constantly in need of money. There is no way of knowing exactly what instructions Elwes received from his masters at this stage, but it could not have been long before their intentions became plain. According to Sir Arthur Wilson, Northampton persuaded Elwes to fall into their plans:

> 'smoothing him with such language, and promising him such rewards, as he thought fittest to gain upon him; assuring him that it would be acceptable service to the King to have him [that is, Overbury] removed, being an insolent and pernicious fellow, of a factious and dangerous spirit; and therefore advised him to be cautious in admitting any to see him, lest his passions should vent themselves and become public.'

In order for their design to be effective it was necessary for the plotters to secure control, not merely of the Tower, but also of the person of Overbury. The day after he took up post, therefore, Elwes, prompted by Sir Thomas Monson, master of the armoury and another of Northampton's clients, appointed Richard Weston to act as Overbury's under-keeper, or gaoler, with the promise of a messenger's job at court. Weston was the sixty-year-old son of an apothecary and a former bailiff to Dr Forman who had formerly worked for Anne Turner. According to Oldisworth, he was, 'A meagre fellow, with a bloodless face pallid as death and a grisled beard, he was cast by nature for the part he was called to play'. Once when caught counterfeiting coin he had barely escaped hanging.

Weston was given strict instructions concerning his prisoner. According to evidence later given in court, Northampton, as chief Secretary of State, ordered that Overbury be kept confined, 'so close, that he scarce had the comfort of the day's brightness; neither suffered he [Northampton] any one to visit him; father, brother, his best friends, his nearest kindred were strangers to him from the beginning of his imprisonment unto the end'. The prisoner was even forbidden to write or receive letters, though this seems to have been a rule which was easily circumvented, at least so far as

Overbury in the Tower

correspondence approved by the plotters was concerned. As we shall see, other letters may have been smuggled in, hidden in food. The fact remained that Overbury was under a degree of restraint far more rigorous than was customary for someone charged with nothing more serious than the crime of contempt. His friend, Sir Robert Killigrew, discovered to his cost just how rigorously he was confined when he visited Sir Walter Raleigh in the Tower along with Overbury's brother in law, Sir John Lidcote. Spotting the prisoner at the window of his cell Killigrew ventured to speak to him and was briefly thrown into the Fleet prison for his pains.

The first person Overbury wrote to for help in his adversity was his 'friend', Carr:

> '... the former accustomed favours and absolute promise concerning my delivery have caused me at this time by these lines to solicit your lordship and to put you in remembrance of the same, not doubting that your honour is at all forgetful of me, but only by reason of my imprisonment, being possessed of a dangerous disease, would for my body's safety, partake of the felicity of the open air: in which case, if your lordship please to commiserate my present necessities, and procure me my speedy delivery, I shall not only stand so much the more obliged, but also acknowledge you the defender and preserver of my life.'[2]

Carr replied to the effect that, though he could not secure Overbury's release immediately, he would soon be able to. In fact, he did nothing, subsequently excusing himself by saying that the King's ear was not ready to entertain any such motion.

As Chief Justice Coke was to remark later, Overbury was now 'a close prisoner to all his friends, but open to all his enemies ...'. Those enemies now began to assail him by mind and by body.

---

[2] *The Harleian Miscellany* (London, 1810).

THE ASSAULTS ON THE MIND

We have a graphic description of how the plotters set about their task. In a letter to Carr, Northampton described how he had 'spent two hours yesterday, prompting the Lieutenant [Elwes] with cautions and considerations; observing with whom he is to deal, that he might the better act his part, for the adventure in which he dealeth'. Elwes in turn wrote to Northampton describing just how diligently he had obeyed his instructions:

> '... I walked with [Overbury] in his chamber, and advised him to give way to the match between Rochester and the Countess; but then he grew hot against your lordship and the Countess of Suffolk [Frances], saying, "If he were the Countess of Suffolk's prisoner," (as he thought he was) then (said he) "let her know that I 'care as little to die as she to be cruel.'" The Countess of Suffolk I find to be joined with you in this plot, though the chamberlain knows not of it, nor anyone else. But Rochester's part I shall much fear, until I see the event to be clearly conveyed.'

But the obstinate Overbury would not budge one inch, and within weeks of entering the Tower he began to sicken. Just why this was we shall examine later.

THE ASSAULTS ON THE BODY

Apparently under the impression that he still enjoyed his former influence with his patron, one of Overbury's first acts on being imprisoned had been to write to Carr demanding food ('You must give order presently and send for wine, jelly and a tart to be brought to me tomorrow ...'). Despite the peremptory language of this request, the Earl obliged by sending in the desired victuals. Soon after, Frances took over the task of supplementing the prisoner's rations, using Simon Merston, a former employee of Sir Thomas Monson, as her go-between. It was the opportunity she had been waiting for.

Overbury in the Tower

The day after Weston had been appointed gaoler (6 May), he set about making the first attempt to poison his prisoner with what we now know to have been red arsenic (or realgar to give it its old name); it was foiled, quite adventitiously, by Elwes himself. Years later the Lieutenant was to describe how it happened:

> 'Not many nights after I had placed him there, Weston did meet me, (the place I am well advised of) and being ready to carry up his soup, asked me whether he should now give him that which he had or no. I presently did withdraw him, not taking any amazement, nor pretending ignorance; but until I had discovered that which I desired, did run the same course with him. When I had obtained that which I desired, I did begin to terrify him with God's eternal judgment, and did so strike him, as with his hands holden up, he blessed the time that ever he did know me, with other words to that effect over long to trouble your Majesty with. "Why sir," (said the fellow) "did you not know what should be done?" I protested my ignorance therein unto him. I would be glad to protest the like in the face of the world. By these means I did get the fellow assured unto me, and understood from time to time whatsoever within his knowledge could be practised against him.'

It had been a close shave for the prisoner.

Overbury, blissfully unaware of the abortive attempt on his life, sought to obtain the King's sympathy by asking to see a doctor on the ground of (unspecified) leg problems. In fact, the problems were of long standing, but he claimed that they were the result of his incarceration. When this request brought no results, Overbury adopted a bolder ruse to gain the King's sympathy; he asked Carr to send him a powder to simulate the symptoms of a stomach disorder. Carr duly obtained the necessary powder from Killigrew and sent it to Overbury by his manservant, Giles Rawlins, who also happened to be Overbury's cousin. It produced no more than a mild diarrhoea (or, as the prisoner put it, 'It worked only with me downward').

But Overbury had another trick up his sleeve: he begged Carr to take the powder himself in order to fool the King into believing that he too was suffering from the same disorder. Surprisingly, Carr agreed to fall in with this plan and swallowed some of the powder, but although the results may have moved him they certainly did not move the King; while expressing sympathy for Carr, James adamantly refused to release Overbury.

On 5 June, Carr sent the prisoner another powder concealed inside a letter in which he had written: 'It will make you more sick, but fear not. I will make that a means for your delivery and for the recovery of your health'. The powder did, indeed, make Overbury worse, much worse. After taking it he experienced diarrhoea on fifty to sixty occasions over the next four days. He also suffered a complete lack of appetite, combined with a raging thirst.

Overbury now began to suspect that things were not as they seemed and wrote to Carr in the bitterest of terms: 'I wonder you have not yet found means to effect my delivery; but I remember you said you would be even with me ... and so indeed you are; but assure yourself, my lord, if you do not release me, but suffer me thus to die, my blood will be required at your hands'. (While Overbury gradually woke up to the fact that he was being deceived by Carr, he never seems to have suspected that Frances had any ill intentions towards him.) Carr's response was to offer to send friends into the Tower to comfort the prisoner, as well as a promise that he would send in meat of better quality.

Overbury seems to have got over this disorder, but by mid-July his health began to decline again, this time seriously. His next letter to Carr described how he had become feverish and that his urine was 'strangely high'. As soon as Overbury's father got to hear of his son's condition he petitioned the King, asking that he should be given medical treatment. James responded immediately by sending his own physician to attend the prisoner.

THE KING'S DOCTOR

Theodore Turquet de Mayerne is an intriguing character. Born in Geneva in 1573 the son of a French Huguenot (or Protestant), he obtained a degree in medicine from the University of Montpellier and soon made a reputation for himself as a fashionable practitioner. By his early twenties his fame was such that he was appointed physician to King Henry IV of France. Religious prejudice led to his being expelled from the French College of Physicians, but it does not seem to have affected his thriving practice. His opportunity to get out of anti-Huguenot France came when he successfully treated a relative of Robert Cecil's travelling in Paris who had been struck down in an epidemic. This led to him being appointed, first as physician to Queen Anne, and later to King James also. He moved to England where he soon built up a fashionable practice and dropped the plebeian-sounding family name of Turquet.

Like most doctors of his day, Mayerne was an alchemist and follower of the Hermetic practitioner, Paracelsus, but he was no narrow minded mediaevalist. His biographer, Hugh Trevor-Roper has described him as 'an open-minded, rational, objective practitioner'. He certainly seems to have been assiduous in his treatment of Overbury. While he was in the Tower his apothecary, Paul de Loubell dispensed 28 sheaves of prescriptions for the patient on his instructions. Sadly, we do not know what they were or what they had been prescribed for. (Some clue as to their strength may be found in Mayerne's favourite saying that 'most often it is the bitterest medicines which work the best'.) But nothing the physician did brought about any improvement in Overbury's condition.

The true depths of his predicament were now beginning to dawn on the increasingly sick prisoner, who approached Carr once again. But instead of supplication he offered reproach, '... for my part I wonder that you [go] abroad and are seen in the world, I lying here, for God refuse me if I be not ashamed of staying here so long that now I never dare to open the windows to look out'. Overbury next wrote to Carr under the pseudonym of Killigrew declaring that, 'I have now sent to the lieutenant to desire you, Mayerus [that is, Mayerne] being absent, to send young Crag [that is Doctor Craig] hither, and Nessmith [Doctor Naismith], if Nessmith be away, send I pray Crag and Allen'. Carr thereupon wrote to one of the doctors, 'Mr Craig, whensoever Sr. Thomas Overbury shall desire you to come to him, the King is pleased you shall go ... I pray you let him have your best help, and as much of your company as he shall require'. Doctors Craig, Naismith and Allen did indeed attend Overbury at various times throughout his incarceration, but his health continued to deteriorate, as one of his letters makes vividly clear, 'This morning (notwithstanding my fasting till yesterday) I find a great heat continew in all my bodye; and the same desire of drinke and loathing of meat, and my water is strangly high, which I keep till Mayerus com'. Despite blood-letting, he wrote, 'my heat slackens nott, my water remains as high, my thirstines the same; the same loathing of meat, having eat not a bitt since thursday was senight to this howre; the same scworing [sic] and vomitting. Yesternight about eight o'clocke, after Mr Mayerus was gone, I faynted and vomited'.[3]

Overbury now began to suffer 'very vehemently ... by vomits and extreme purging'.[4] His father, who had been refused access to his son, turned once more to the Earl. Carr's response was to warn him not to interfere, but to stay in the country. Nothing was to be gained, he wrote, by pestering the King, and to do so might 'stir

---

[3] Quoted in Edward F. Rimbault, Ll.D. (ed.), *The Miscellaneous Works in Prose and Verse of Sir Thomas Overbury Knt., Now First Collected* (London, John Russell Smith, 1856). Once again, the letter was written under the pseudonym of his friend, Killigrew, possibly in order to get around the restrictions on his correspondence.

[4] Lawrence Hyde at the Earl's trial.

up his enemies' and prejudice his chances of release. He wrote in similar terms to Overbury's mother, promising that 'Before your coming home you shall hear he is a free man'. It was a distasteful lie from the man who had plotted their son's incarceration.

Meanwhile, Frances continued to send poisoned food in to the prisoner. When on 10 July he expressed a fancy for tarts and jellies, they were duly brought in by Anne Turner 'with the knowledge of the ... Countess'.[5] Upon eating them he is said to have experienced 'the extremity of sickness'. But nothing in Overbury's last days seemed to go as expected and shortly afterwards, to everyone's surprise and presumably Frances' dismay, he began to regain his health. Not knowing what to make of this and fearing that Weston had not been following her instructions, the Countess sent for him and demanded action.

'STANDING BETWIXT HOPE AND FEAR'

Elwes now redoubled his efforts to make Overbury withdraw his objection to the annulment. In late August, acting on instructions from Northampton, he told him that his only hope of freedom lay in obtaining the favour of Suffolk (Thomas Howard) who, he assured him, had been seeking to intervene with the King on his behalf. The pressure which Overbury was now under is apparent from Elwes' frank report to Northampton:

'My special good lord,

Having undertook my prisoner according to your instructions, after long silence, as standing betwixt hope and fear, he takes his bible, and after he had read upon it, laid it by and protested his innocency, afterward upon further conference concerning the

---

[5] In Weston's indictment the 10 July attempt was recorded as 19 July.

Countess, he said that he had justified her already, and that he can do no more than what he had done already.

But for myself, alas, (quoth he) what will they do with me? I answered, so reason you as you shall make no question hereafter of your pureness. And I left him in some sense to work upon him; as I was going, he concluded that in the generality she was so worthy that she might be a wife in particular for my lord of Rochester [Carr], he would not say it, lest my lord should condemn him for weighing his worth.

At my next coming to him, I found him, not in sense, but in fury, he let fly at you, but was respective [respectful] to my lord of Rochester whose part he took altogether; I see the event, I desire it may be safely carried, what my service may do in this or any thing else, I will be faithful to your lordship, and so I rest,

Yours, Jervis Elwes.'[6]

The relentless pressure finally had its desired effect: Overbury broke and agreed to beg Suffolk for help. But the letter he wrote was in half-hearted terms. When Elwes pressed him to adopt a more supplicant posture, Overbury agreed to 'write with a fuller pen', and his next letter (of 20 August) expressed his gratitude at the Earl's supposed assistance and undertook to 'endeavour to the uttermost of my friendship to continue that friendship between your two Lordships [that is Suffolk and Carr] firm and inviolable'. It was exactly what the plotters had been hoping for and produced an immediate response from Suffolk in which he undertook to continue to use his influence with the King to secure Overbury's release, albeit coupled with a warning that this might 'be a work of some time'.

---

[6] 'Truth brought to Light by Time, or the History of the first 14 years of King James 1', p. 58, quoted in a footnote to *The State Trials*.

An overjoyed Overbury replied at once expressing his regret at having 'been a stranger thus long unto your Lordship'. Pushing his luck just a bit further he wrote that, while his health had improved, only a change of air would allow it to be fully restored. In his euphoria, the prisoner dashed off letters to his relatives with the news that he hoped to be released in a week or ten days. He wrote in similar terms to Carr, blissfully unaware that it was he who had been orchestrating the correspondence throughout.

The day after Suffolk's letter (24 August) Overbury, desperate to mend fences all round and no doubt under continuing pressure from Elwes, wrote to Northampton offering the ultimate concession, an apology to Frances; or at any rate the nearest he ever came to one:

> 'Tis true, my very good Lord, that I have heard from many, yea from my Lord Rochester himself, with what bitterness her Ladyship would often speak of me, and out of the sense of that *'tis possible I may have* spoken with less respect of her than was fit, but that ever I touched her in point of her honour, far be it from me. For I protest 'twas never in my words nor in my belief, and this I will profess to all the world. And if either my Lady of Suffolk or the Lady herself shall rest unsatisfied, I will be ready to tender as much to their Ladyships and to say the same which now I write to your Lordship; and for my Lady of Essex, *if I might be only freed from her ill-will for time to come*, there shall be no man readier to respect and honour her than myself.' (Emphasis added)

It was a less than handsome apology, compounded almost immediately by a characteristic piece of ill judgement. Unbelievably in light of his circumstances, Overbury now wrote to Carr begging him once again not to marry Frances. On learning of this, Northampton could not contain himself and in a letter to Carr expressed doubts about the prisoner's health, concluding sinisterly that 'either (he) shall recover, and do good offices betwixt my lord of Suffolk and you; which if he do not, you shall have reason to count him a knave: or else, that he shall not recover at all, which he thinks the most sure and happy change of all'.[7] A contemporary wrote that 'it would turn chaste blood into water to hear the unchaste and unclean phrases that were contained' in Northampton's letters to Carr.[8]

Overbury, though far from popular, was not entirely friendless; his brother-in-law, Lidcote had been pressing for some time to visit him in the Tower. When finally permitted to do so he 'found him very sick in his bed, his hand dry, his speech hollow'. His fears were compounded when Overbury asked his visitor to draw up a will for him. As Sir John was preparing to leave, the prisoner asked softly whether Carr 'juggled with him or not'. Lidcote said he thought not; it was an opinion that he soon came to revise.

In his next conversation with Carr, Lidcote noted that, when his brother-in-law's name was mentioned, the Earl gave 'a counterfeit sigh and ... at that instant he smiled in my face'. It was enough for him to realize that Carr 'dealt not plainly with him', and he wrote at once urging Overbury to get out of the Tower by whatever means he might. He warned, '[N]ever was man so cozened as you are ... there is no honest quarter to be had with him'. He also mentioned that Carr had complained of the prisoner's 'unreverend' style when addressing him. All Overbury could think to do was to Carr demanding to know why:

> 'With what face could you tell him that you would be less to me, to whom you owe more than to any Soule living, both for your Fortune, Understanding and Reputation? ... Alas this shift will not serve to cover your vow, your sacrificing me to your Woman, your holding a firm friendship with those that brought me hither and keep me heare, and not make it your first act of any good terms with them to set me free and restore me to yourself againe.'

[7] Andrew Amos, *The Great Oyer of Poisoning: The Trial of the Earl of Somerset for the possible poisoning of Sir Thomas Overbury* (London, Richard Bentley, 1846).
[8] John Castle. Letter.

Overbury in the Tower

The prisoner's rising anger led him on to describe in long and rambling terms a complex (and almost certainly imaginary) plan he had devised to wreak his revenge:

> 'I have all this Vacation wrote the story betwixt you and me from the first Hower to this day ... how many hazards I have runn for you ... what secrets have passed betwixt you and me ... how when you fell in love with that woman, as soon as you had won her by my letters ... Thereupon you made your vow that I should live in the court, was my friend and many oathes which are now fulfilled; stayed me here when I should have ben gone, and sent for me twice in that day that I was caught in the trap ...
>
> All these particulars I have set down in a large discourse, and on Tuesday I made an end of wrighting it fair, and on Friday I have sealed it under eight Seales, and sent it by a friend of myne whom I dare trust (taking his oath not to open it) I send to him, and then to all my friends Noble and Gentelmen and Women and then to read it to them and take copies of it, and I vowed to have wrote the truthe. ... I have provided that whether I die or live your nature shall never die, nor leave to be the most odious man alive.'[9]

If only this precaution had been carried out in reality and not just in the prisoner's imagination. The plotters' response was to remove the prisoner to a smaller cell and forbid him to receive any more letters. His health now took a serious turn for the worse, as reflected in his shaky handwriting of the time, and a seemingly anxious Carr wrote to Mayerne, then in Bath, seeking his advice. The doctor replied saying that if the prisoner were to write to him describing his symptoms he might be able to find out what was wrong with him. We do not know whether this offer of 'distance diagnosis' was ever taken up.

Overbury made his last plea to Carr on or about 13 September, only two days before he died. It was in pitiable terms, 'Is this the fruit of my care and love to you? Be these the fruits of common

---

[9] Letter of 27 August, in *Memorials,* Vol. III, p. 478.

Passion, Poison and Power

secrets, common dangers? As a man you cannot suffer me to lie in this misery; yet your behaviour betrays you. All I intent of you is that you will free me from this place; and that we may part friends'.

Characteristically, he could not resist adding, 'Drive me not to extremities, lest I should say something that you and I both repent'. Overbury had no time to carry out his threat for after much vomiting and purging he died at about five o'clock in the morning of 15 September 1613. He was hastily buried in the choir of the Tower chapel of Saint Peter ad Vincula between three and four p.m. the same day, nearly five months after he had entered that grim prison.[10]

Shortly afterwards, Carr wrote to the dead man's father to commiserate with him for the loss of his son.

'LET THE PRIEST BE READY'

Elwes was now faced with the dilemma of disposing of the body of a man he must have believed, or at the very least suspected, was the victim of murder. Fortunately for posterity, he recorded how he dealt with the situation in a note endorsed on the back of a letter from Northampton:

> 'So soon as Sir Thomas Overbury was departed I writ unto my Lord of Northampton; and because my experience could not direct me I desired to know what I should do with the body, acquainting his Lordship with the issues [that is, discharges], as Weston had informed me and other foulness of his body, which then was accounted the pox. My Lord writ unto me that I should first have his body viewed by a jewery; and I well remember his Lordship advised me to send for Sir John Lidcote to see the body and to suffer

---

[10] Charles Edward Gough argues that the chapel was too small to take the burial and points out that the relevant register entry was made years later (*Life and Characters of Sir Thomas Overbury*).

as many of his friends to see of it as would and presently to bury it in the body of the quire, for the body could not keep.

Notwithstanding Sir Thomas Overbury dying about five in the morning I kept his body unburied until three or four of the clock in the afternoon. The next day Sir John Lidcote came thither; and I could not get him to bestow a coffin nor a winding sheet upon him. The coffin I bestowed; but who did wind him I know not. For indeed the body was very noisome; so that notwithstanding my Lord's direction by reason of the danger of keeping the body, I kept it overlong, as we all felt.'

What had happened was that as soon as Northampton learned of Overbury's death he had written to Elwes telling him that Carr wished to be given the body of his deceased friend 'in order to do him honour at his funeral'. He declared that he could see no impediment to this 'honourable desire of my Lord's but the unsweetness of the body because it was reported that he had some issues [that is, discharges], and in that case the keeping of him above [ground] must needs give more offence than it can do honour. My fear', the letter went on, 'is also that the body is already buried upon that cause whereof I write; which being so it is too late to set solemnity'. It could not have been a broader hint to the Lieutenant to act swiftly in disposing of the embarrassing cadaver.

Within hours of writing that letter, Northampton sent another instructing the Lieutenant to call Lidcote and three or four of the dead man's friends to view the body, after which, he wrote, it should be buried 'instantly' within the body of the Tower chapel. That 'damned crew's only desire', he wrote, was 'to move pity and raise scandals'. The letter ended, 'Fail not a jote herein as you love your friends; nor after Lidcote and his friends have viewed stay one minute, but let the priest be ready; and if Lidcote be not there, send for him speedily, *pretending* that the body will not tarry'. [Emphasis added.] This missive, which was marked, 'Posthaste at 12', contained the incriminating injunction 'Bring me these letters when I next see you'. (This instruction was obviously not followed, but when the truth came to light it was too late to embarrass its author.)

Despite these instructions, Elwes did call a coroner, Robert Bright, to view the body, a circumstance which has given rise to some confusion. Bright was one of the Middlesex coroners, but Overbury had died in a part of the Tower that was in the City rather than the town of London.[11] Bright failed to return his verdict to the King's Bench, as he should have done, and was later to excuse his neglect on the ground that he did not want the City of London to have any ground for action against him. It was hardly a convincing explanation. But what was the finding of coroner Bright's court? Sir Simonds D'Ewes asserted that it was one of natural death, but we have nothing to corroborate this.

Meanwhile, the cause for which Overbury had been thrown into the Tower in the first place was approaching its fruition.

---

[11] Writing of this case in his *Institutes*, Coke explained that 'the ancient wall of London ... extendeth through the Tower of London; and all that which is on the West part of the Wall is within the City of London, ... : and all that is on the East part of the Wall is in the County of Middlesex; and the Chamber of Sir Thomas Overbury was within the Tower on the West part of the said Wall, and therefore Weston was tried within the City of London'.

ACT 5

'THE GALLANT MASQUE OF LORDS'

The Commission which had been appointed to consider Frances' petition (or 'libel', as it was called in law) for nullity of marriage consisted of four bishops and six judges under the chairmanship of George Abbot, Archbishop of Canterbury. It first convened at Lambeth palace on 16 May 1613, just three weeks after Overbury had begun his incarceration in the Tower.[1]

Frances' petition alleged in accordance with the agreed plan that:

> 'since the pretended Marriage, at least by the space of whole continuate three years after the said Robert had fully attained the age of eighteen years [the couple] lay both naked and alone in the same bed, as married folk use and, desirous to be made a mother, from time to time, again and again [Frances] yielded herself to his power, and as much as lay in her offered herself and her body to be known ... [but, it went on] the Earl never carnally knew her [despite the fact that he] hath power and ability to deal with other women and to know them carnally.'

The Archbishop was a conscientious, though somewhat narrow minded man. He had been asked to chair the Commission only

---

[1] The following account of the nullity proceedings is based upon *The State Trials* report.

four days before it began its hearings and the unusual grounds for the application came as a complete surprise to him and his colleagues: 'When we saw it', he wrote in his private records, 'and that it contained *"impotentia versus hanc"* [that it to say, impotence limited to a particular woman], most of us, who were not acquainted with the project before, were much amazed at it'. In his view there was no lawful precedent for such an action. Indeed, Frances' lawyers had had to go back to the thirteenth-century writings of Saint Thomas Aquinas to discover even tenuous authority for the notion of selective incompetence which, it was believed, could only be brought about by witchcraft. It was not surprising that Abbott should have warned Frances' counsel that they had 'laid a very narrow bridge for themselves to go over'.

In his written 'Answer' Robert claimed that 'when he was willing, [Frances] shewed herself sometimes willing, but other times refused, and he lay in bed most commonly with her, but felt no motions or provocations'. '[B]efore and after the Marriage', the Answer went on, 'he hath found an ability of body to know any other woman, and hath oftentimes felt motions and provocations of the flesh tending to carnal copulation, ... but that he hath lain by the lady Frances two or three years last past, and had no motion to know her, and he believes never shall'. Apparently throwing aside the secret agreement, the Answer went on to claim that its author 'believeth not that the said lady Frances is a woman able and fit for carnal copulation, because he hath not found it'. Frances, however, stuck to her part of the bargain by claiming that:

> '[S]ince the earl of Essex was 18 years of age he and I have for the space of three years divers and sundry times lain together in naked bed all night. And at sundry of the said times the said earl hath purposely endeavoured and attempted to consummate marriage with me, and to have carnal copulation with me for procreation of children: and I have at such times, as the said earl hath attempted so to do, yielded myself willing to the same purpose.'

'The Gallant Masque of Lords'

So much for the preliminaries: the hearing proper began with Frances appearing in person to affirm her petition on oath. (She had to be prompted by one of her brothers to sign as 'Frances Howard' and not 'Frances Essex', forgetting that she was alleging that her marriage had never taken place at law.[2]) A number of witnesses, servants and friends were called upon to prove the lack of consummation, even though it was not in dispute, and Frances' father, Thomas Howard, deposed on oath that Essex had admitted his impotence to him.

In a 'Memorial' written by Dr Abbott and published in *The State Trials*, Essex is quoted as telling the Commission bluntly, 'When I came out of France I loved her; I do not now; neither ever shall I'. When asked to respond to the claim that Frances was a virgin, he smiled and said, 'She saith so, and she is for [that is, towards] me'. It was the plainest of hints that his wife had committed adultery. Faced with this conflict of evidence and given the uncertain state of the law the Commissioners could not, despite lengthy and often acrimonious debate, agree among themselves. A minority declared themselves unable to find anything in the scriptures which would authorize an annulment. Foremost among them was the chairman, who took the view that Essex' impotence was 'for lack of love, and not for want of ability'. His naïve suggestion that the parties might consider conciliation predictably came to naught.

But the proceedings were not moving as swiftly as the King desired. When on 18 June the Commissioners put the case off for over a fortnight, he summoned their chairman to a private meeting at which he made his dissatisfaction known. Abbot responded by saying that the adjournment was necessary for the convenience of the lawyers, but James made it plain that he did not think this reason enough.

---

[2] Unlike divorce, annulment does not put an end to a marriage; it simply declares that it has never taken place.

When the Commissioners adjourned once again a furious James summoned them all to Windsor. After addressing them sternly on their lack of progress he took Abbot aside and told him bluntly that if he and his colleagues were to vote against the petition 'we must either begin all again and have a new libel or we must have a new Commission'. But when the Commissioners reconvened the next day they were no nearer agreement.

Abbot was a worried man. As he privately recorded, he had:

> 'heard many strange stories of the lady's carriage. Something was freely spoken of a woman arraigned at Bury [possibly Toothless Margaret]; and how to shut that up, and so to free the Earl, this course was consented upon. These things, though out of charity I entertained not as absolutely true, yet the concurrence of them from so many, made me that I could not contemn them. Besides, now grew the rumour strong, that a new husband was readily provided for her.'

Carr's role in Frances' love life had obviously reached the Archbishop's ears.

Abbott was particularly disturbed at the King's seeming lack of impartiality and in a frank note to himself wrote,

> 'What a strange and fearful thing it was that his Majesty should be so engaged in that business; that he should profess that himself had set the matter in that course of judgement; that the judges should be dealt withall beforehand, and in a sort directed what they should determine'.

Reluctantly coming to the conclusion that he could not in all conscience do the King's bidding, he wanted nothing less than to be excused from taking part in the charade, offering the excuse that, as a bachelor, he was not fitted for the task. He prayed 'humbly that I might be freed from the trouble of this cause, or, at least, give no sentence in it till I were a married man, and so might better understand the business'. His request met with a dusty answer, which prompted Abbot to set out his 'scruples' in the form of a draft judgment refusing the annulment.

James, who was not without learning in these matters, was enraged. Determined to see the marriage ended, he wrote to the Archbishop stating at length his reasons for believing that the proceedings were justified in canon law. The letter, which James allowed to become public, concluded with a monumental put-down:

> 'I must freely confess that I find the grounds of your opposition so weak, as I have reason to apprehend that the prejudice you have of the persons is the greatest motive of breeding these doubts into you; which prejudice is the most dangerous thing that can fall in a judge for misleading of his mind. [This was a reference to the strongly anti-Catholic Abbot's aversion to the Catholic-leaning Howards.] It should become you rather to have a kind of faith implicit in my judgment, as well in respect of some skill I have in divinity, as also that I hope no honest man doubts of the uprightness of my conscience; and the best thankfulness that you, that are so far my creature, can use towards me, is, to reverente and follow my judgment, and not to contradict it, except when you may demonstrate unto me that I am mistaken or wrong informed. And so farewell.'

By now, Frances' affair with Carr had become common knowledge. Belatedly realizing that the proceedings were probably collusive (and thus illegal), the Commissioners ordered that an examination should be carried out to determine whether the petitioner was still a virgin and appointed six midwives 'of the best note' and four 'noble matrons' for the purpose. These ladies duly carried out an examination and reported that Frances was *'virgo intacta et incorrupta'* [virgin intact and uncorrupted]. Their conclusion gave rise to much immoderate amusement. Weldon, for example, dryly remarked that the outcome of the examination 'was thought very strange, for the world took notice that her way was very near beaten so plain, ... and in truth, was a common way before Somerset did ever travel that way; besides, the world took notice they two long had lived in Adultery'. Even the late Prince Henry had been aware of her reputation. The tale goes that once, when handed a glove worn by her, he had rejected it as having been 'stretched by another'.[3]

How then did the examiners – effectively the midwives because the noble matrons considered the task beneath them – get it so wrong? One explanation, as the historian Anne Somerset observed in her book on Overbury, is that it is difficult even today to establish through physical examination whether a woman is a virgin or not.[4] The editors of *The State Trials,* never ones for letting the possibility of a scandal go unnoticed, came up with an altogether more dramatic scenario which they ascribed to 'some authors'. This claimed that 'the Countess under a pretence of modesty, having obtained leave to put on a veil when she was inspected, caused a young woman of her age and stature and dressed in her clothes to stand the search in her place'. Weldon, who was one of the main sources for this rumour, sought to confirm it with a particularly circuitous piece of hearsay, 'If any make doubt of the truth of this story, the author delivers upon the reputation of S.W.B. a gentleman, he had it verbatim from a knight, otherwise of much honor, though the very dependency on that family may question it, which did usher the lady into the place of inspection, and hath told it often to his friends in mirth'.

Strange as it may seem and despite its dubious provenance, the story of the substituted virgin could actually be true. The idea that the Countess should be examined had come from her side, not

---

[3] Sir Simonds D'Ewes in James Orchard Halliwell (ed.), *Letters of the Kings of England now first collected from Royal Archives and other Authentic Sources, Private as well as Public*, Vol. I (London, Henry Colburn, 1848), p. 90.

[4] Anne Somerset, *Unnatural Murder: Poison in the Court of King James I* (London, Weidenfeld & Nicolson, 1997).

from his: her supporters must have been well aware of Frances' promiscuous reputation and would never have suggested a test of virginity without being confident of the outcome. Counsel for Essex did what he could to challenge the result of the examination, but without success. But the public were not deceived, as a piece of doggerel of the time suggests:

> 'There was at court a Lady of late
> That none could enter she was so straight
> But now with use shee is grow so wide
> There is a passage for a Carr to ride.'[5]

Even the Commissioners were unconvinced by the declaration of virginity, for on 18 September they announced their intention to adjourn the hearing in order that Essex could be recalled to give further evidence. It was a prevarication too far for a furious James, who stepped in to forbid the proposed adjournment (ostensibly on the ground that it would be unfair) and instructed the court to come to its decision by 25 September at the latest. He also summoned Abbot in order to impress upon him once again the need for his Commission to arrive at the 'correct' verdict. It disturbed the Archbishop who noted his private misgivings that 'all was not right', 'Good Lord! What a case is this? Shall any truth be kept from us? Are they afraid to have all out? Do they only look to attain their own end, and care not how our consciences be entangled and ensnared?'

Abbot made one last plea to be relieved of his burden, reportedly on his knees, but it was doomed to failure: the Commissioners had to give way to the King's demands. Accordingly, on the appointed day they declared the marriage of Frances and Essex to be 'utterly void and none effect' on the ground that the Earl 'by some secret,

---

[5] *Poems on Affairs of State: Augustan Satirical Verse, 1660–1714*, William J. Cameron (ed.) Vol. V: 1688–1697 (New Haven, Yale University Press, 1972).

incurable, binding impediment, did never carnally know or was or is able carnally to know the Lady Frances Howard'. We can only speculate what the court's decision would have been if it had been aware of the fact that, throughout the time the couple were living and sleeping together, Frances was taking determined steps, natural and supernatural, to reduce her husband's libido.

The Commission's decision was a majority one from which Abbot and five others abstained. And it had been engineered – quite improperly – by the King, who had made sure of the right verdict by appointing two additional commissioners known to be favourable to the petition and adjusting the quorum rule in favour of the finding he desired. He even took steps to muzzle the Commissioners. On the morning of their 'sentence' (as it was called) the Commissioners had unwisely announced their intention to explain why they had voted as they did: a scandalized James put a stop to this tardy expression of independence by ordering them to announce their verdicts without explanation.

And so it was that on Boxing Day 1613, nearly eight years after Frances' wedding to Essex, the Countess joyfully married her lover, Robert Carr, now elevated to the rank and title of Earl of Somerset and Baron Brancepeth in order that his social status should not be inferior to that of his wife's. It seemed to be a win all round: Frances had got her annulment and Essex, the man's man, had successfully defended his virility, at least with respect to women in general. (His delight was somewhat marred by the fact that he had to repay the £6,000 dowry which he had received upon his marriage to Frances.)

The celebration of Frances' second marriage was an even grander event than that of the first, though not in every respect as successful.

FRANCES' SECOND MARRIAGE

The ceremony took place in the Chapel Royal, Whitehall, the scene of the first wedding, the same bishop of Bath and Wells officiating. Almost as if she were defying her critics, the bride, who had 'grown to be a beauty of the greatest magnitude in the horizon of the Court', was married 'in her hair', that is to say with her tresses hanging down loose almost to her feet, the mark of a virgin.[6] That evening an entertainment was performed in the Banqueting House entitled *The Gallant Masque of Lords*.[7] It started an hour before midnight and ended in the early hours of the morning. Based on a story by the Roman author, Catullus concerning the marriage of Peleus and Thetis, the masque had been written by the poet and composer, Thomas Campion, the strait laced Ben Jonson having jibbed at writing a second wedding masque for the same bride. Unlike the entertainment at the first wedding, the all too visible stage mechanics failed to work properly and were a source of unintended amusement, for which Campion had to apologize profusely.

Once again, sumptuous gifts flowed in to the happy couple. The King gave them £12,000, together with a jewel worth £3,000, immense sums in those days, and the Queen donated 'silver dishes curiously enamelled'. Northampton crowned his achievement in bringing the pair together by a gift of £1,500 in plate, together with an elaborate sword for the groom. Sir Edward Coke sought to ingratiate himself with the present of a basin and cover of silver gilt, while his Lady donated a pot of gold. The Corporation of the City of London, the East India Company, the Merchant Adventurers and the Farmers of the Customs were said to have vied with each other in the costliness of their offerings.

---

[6] Arthur Wilson, *History of Great Britain, Being the Life and Reign of King James I* (1653).
[7] Four out of the twelve were said to have danced in the Masque of Hymen at the former wedding.

Three days after the wedding, a second masque was performed before the King in honour of the marriage. It was Ben Jonson's *The Irish Masque at Court, by Gentlemen the King's Servants*. Six days later Frances and Robert rode in a triumphal procession along Cheapside to the Merchant Tailors' hall, where they were entertained by the Lord Mayor of London. Their carriage was drawn by a team of thoroughbred horses which Sir Ralph Winwood had insisted on providing. Anxious to obtain Carr's support for his appointment as Secretary, he attended the ceremony dressed in an extravagantly costly suit. But even this was not the end.

Yet another entertainment, *The Masque of Flowers*, was performed on Twelfth Night by members of Gray's Inn at the expense of the sycophantic Bacon. The versifiers too contributed their part, most notably John Donne, a client of Carr's, who wrote a poem specially for the occasion.[8] It apostrophized the bridegroom in the contemporary metaphysical style for, 'having laid down in thy Sovereign's breast /All businesses, from thence to reinvest / Them when these triumphs cease, thou forward art /To show to her, who doth the like impart, /The fire of thy inflaming eyes, and of thy loving heart'. The great poet had been suffering from eye trouble and the poem arrived late; it was never acknowledged.[9]

Shortly after the marriage Anne Turner received her reward when she moved into the Countess' household, probably as some form of companion. (She was careful to insist later that she was never a servant.)

Six months later Northampton died of a tumour and post-operative complications: a positive Merry-Go-Round of offices ensued. His nephew Suffolk succeeded him as Lord Treasurer. Carr took Northampton's place as Lord Privy Seal and warden of

---

[8] Eclogue (1613).
[9] John Stubbs, *Donne: The Reformed Soul* (London, Penguin, 2006).

the Cinque Ports and later that year succeeded Suffolk as Lord Chamberlain. The Howard family and their hangers-on were now the unchallenged leaders at court below the Crown. Carr's patronage, at its height, has been estimated at some £90,000 a year.[10] It was now truly said that, 'Nothing of any moment is done here but by [Carr's] mediation'.[11] Even his marriage seemed to be a true love match.

But even at the height of Carr and Frances' power and happiness, events were taking place which would end with their dramatic downfall.

[10] Samuel R. Gardiner, *History of England from the Accession of James I to the Outbreak of the Civil War, 1603–1642,* Vol. 2 (London, Longman, Green and Co, 1883).
[11] Norman E. McClure (ed.),*The Letters of John Chamberlain* (Philadelphia, American Philosophical Society, 1939).

ACT 6

A NEW STAR RISES

Though his patronage was widely sought, Carr was not a popular man. People cared little about his enriching himself at the expense of others – it was only to be expected at court – but he put their backs up by promising advancement for cash and failing to live up to his word. His marriage into the Catholic-leaning Howard family was a cause for resentment among the Protestant faction; and many individuals had their own grievances. Pembroke was aggrieved at having been passed over for the post of Lord Chamberlain, Archbishop Abbot felt ill-used in the matter of the nullity suit and Winwood was still smarting at having for so long been denied the post of Secretary. In time, a number of the disaffected got together at Baynards Castle in the City of London, where they formed a plan to detach Carr from the King. Their idea was to find an alternative Favourite for James with the dual advantages in their eyes of being both English and untainted by any suspicion of Catholicism. Fortunately for them, someone was at hand who suited their purpose better than they could have hoped.

George Villiers had been brought up by his mother, the widow of an impoverished Leicester gentleman. He was a handsome fellow with dark chestnut curly hair, a pointed beard of golden brown, clear skin, chiselled features, blue eyes, and a graceful carriage. He was also skilled in dancing, fencing and riding. In August 1614, the twenty-two-year-old Villiers, recently out of a

A New Star Rises

French finishing school, was introduced to the forty-seven-year-old King. He appeared to James to be 'the most handsomest-bodied man of England; his limbs were so well compacted, and his conversation so pleasing and of so sweet a disposition. And truly his intellectuals were very great; he had sound judgement and was of a quick apprehension'.[1] The reference to 'intellectuals' was perhaps an exaggeration, but there was no doubt about Villiers' charm. The effect the new Favourite had on James was even greater than that of the old.

James now began showering honours and wealth upon the new object of his affections, but when he announced his intention of making the young man a groom of the bedchamber it was too much for Carr, who stepped in to insist that the appointment be given to his cousin instead. James caved in to his wishes, but side stepped them neatly by making Villiers a cup-bearer, a position which placed him in just as close proximity to the throne as if he had been a groom.

As soon as they saw which way the wind was blowing there was no shortage of courtiers willing to provide the young man with all that he needed by way of dress and opportunities. Weldon relates how:

> 'the court rallied to his cause, some assuring him a greater fortune was coming to him; then one gave him his place of cup-bearer, that he might be in the King's eye; another sent to his mercer and taylor to put good cloathes on him; a third to his sempster for curious linnen, and all as incomes to obtain offices upon his future rise; then others tooke upon them to be his bravoes, to undertake his quarrells upon affronts put upon him by Somersets faction: so all hands helped to the piecing up this new Favourite.'

Bacon, that great place server, wrote to the new man, unctuously pledging that, 'I am yours, surer to you than my own life'. It was

---

[1] Godfrey Goodman, *The Court of James I* (London, R. Bentley, 1839).

said that the King now began, 'to eat abroad, who formerly used to eat in his bed-chamber, or if by chance supped in his bed-chamber, after supper would come forth to see pastimes and fooleries'.

Villiers was knighted in April 1615 at a ceremony held, significantly, in the Queen's bedchamber. At the same time he was given a massive pension of £1,000 a year and appointed gentleman of the bedchamber, skipping the usual stage of groom. If there is doubt about the physical nature of James' relations with Carr, none can be possible in the case of Villiers whom the King kissed openly on the lips and was known to describe as his Queen.

The new Favourite's standing at court was now plain for all to see. Carr was incandescent with rage. Unwisely, he did nothing to conceal it from the King.

JAMES' COMPLAINT

We can tell exactly how badly Carr reacted to being sidelined in the King's affections from an extraordinary letter which James felt compelled to write rebuking him. Carr, he complained, 'deserved more trust and confidence of me than ever man did, in secrecy above all flesh, in feeling and impartial respect, as well to my honour in every degree as to my profit'. Although the 'trust and privacy' between the two of them had given Carr an 'infinitely great liberty and freedom of speech unto me' than other men; he had abused that liberty by rebuking his monarch 'more bitterly and sharply than ever my master durst do'.

Carr, James went on, had taken to railing at him 'at unseasonable hours, and so bereaving me of my rest'. (The letter referred to 'unseasonable hours' three times and to James' want of rest twice.) He mentioned Carr's 'fiery boutades' (impulsive conceits) and 'continual dogged sullen behaviour', and charged him with doubting the King's friendship; worst of all, with having, 'in many

A New Star Rises

of your mad fits done what you can to persuade me that you mean not so much to hold me by love as by awe, and that you have me so far in your reverence, as that I dare not offend you, or resist your appetites. ... I leave out of this reckoning', the letter went on, 'your long creeping back and withdrawing yourself from lying in my chamber, notwithstanding my many hundred times earnestly soliciting you to the contrary ...'.

James had borne his grief as long as he could: all he desired, he wrote, was that Carr should be kind to him. Most particularly, he should stop attempting to overawe his monarch. The letter concluded with a crushing reproof:

> 'Remember that all your being, except your breathing and soul, is from me. I told you twice or thrice, you might lead me by the heart and not by the nose ... A King may slack a part of his affection towards his servant upon the party's default, and yet love him; but a servant cannot do so to his master, but his master must hate him ... Do not all courtesies and places come through your office as chamberlain, and rewards through your father-in-law as treasurer? Do not you two (as it were) hedge in all the court with a manner of necessity to depend upon you? And have you not besides your infinite privacy with me, together with all the main offices you possess? — your nephew in my bedchamber?[2] — besides another far more active than he in court-practices? And have you not one of your nearest kinsmen that loves not to be idle in my son's bedchamber?'[3]

This letter has been described as perhaps the strangest that was ever addressed to a subject by a sovereign.[4] As the historian,

---

[2] Carr's nephew had at his request been made a groom of the bedchamber, though what the reference to idleness meant goodness knows.
[3] James Orchard Halliwell (ed.), *Letters of the Kings of England now first collected from Royal Archives and other Authentic Sources, Private as well as Public* (London, Henry Colburn, 1848).
[4] Samuel R. Gardiner, *History of England from the Accession of James I to the Outbreak of the Civil War, 1603–1642,* Vol. 2 (London, Longman, Green and Co, 1883), p. 320.

Alastair Bellany wrote of it, 'Though artfully constructed as a "mirror" for Carr's better understanding, the letter crackles with intense, and seemingly genuine, emotional hurt'.[5] But Carr ignored the King's advice and continued with his foolish recriminations. In the early summer of 1615, James was forced to write again to his one-time Favourite complaining of his 'desperate letters' and pleading that 'if ye do but the half of your duty unto me, ye may be with me in the old manner only by expressing that love to my person and respect to your master that God and man craves of you, with a hearty feeling and penitence of your by-past errors'. Carr seems to have learned nothing from this, except perhaps the need to protect his flank: he set about applying for a royal pardon. It was a step he was to come to regret.

No one can be sure why Carr embarked on this course. The Venetian ambassador surmised that he was concerned about rumours then circulating of his having appropriated some of the Crown jewels, but there seems to be nothing in this story. Carr himself was to plead that he had been involved in dangerous and delicate affairs of State. '[H]aving had many things of trust under the King, and the custody of both the seals, without particular warrant, I desired by this means to be exonerated'. To be fair, precautionary pardons were not unknown in those days; indeed, they were actually recommended in a manual for aspiring courtiers. The ever generous James acceded to the request and directed that a pardon should be drawn up. To the dismay of both men, the Solicitor General refused to certify it on the ground that it was unlawful and without precedent, a view which the Lord Chancellor confirmed, even in face of the King's displeasure. When the Queen

---

[5] Alastair James Bellany, *The Politics of Court Scandal in Early Modern England: News Culture and the Overbury Affair, 1603–1660* (Cambridge, Cambridge University Press, 2002).

A New Star Rises

lent her support to the Chancellor's objection, the King reluctantly agreed that the pardon should be refused.

A month or two later, Carr renewed his request, this time in the form of a new draft the terms of which were wider in scope than the first and which, significantly as some were to believe, specifically mentioned the crime of murder. Events overtook this second request for a pardon which never came to be ruled upon. It was unfortunate for the Earl when the whole business of the pardons came to be portrayed later as his attempts to have himself absolved of responsibility for Overbury's murder.

Nevertheless, James did everything he could to mollify the disgruntled Carr. During a royal progress, in the course of which he seems to have shared a bed with Villiers for the first time, James took steps to bring about a reconciliation between the old and the new Favourites.[6] An intermediary, Sir Humphrey May, was sent to Carr with a gesture of reconciliation. 'My Lord, Sir George Villiers will come to you', he said, 'to offer his service, and desire to be your creature; and therefore refuse him not, embrace him, and your Lordship shall still stand a great man, though not the sole Favorite'. Half an hour later Villiers arrived to make that very declaration. Despite the fact that Carr was well aware that James was behind the offer, he spurned it with the utmost contempt. 'I will none of your service and you shall none of my favour. I will, if I can, break your neck and of that be confident'. It was a reaction which in Weldon's words 'savoured more of spirit than wisdom'.

---

[6] Villiers later referred in a letter to James to 'the time which I shall never forget at Farnham, where the bed's head could not be found between the master and his dog'.

HOW IT ALL CAME OUT

At the time of Overbury's death, no one other than members of his own family was unduly concerned as to how it had come about. There had, it is true, been talk of poison, but this had been countered by rumours, probably encouraged by his enemies, that the prisoner had died a sordid death of the French pox, or syphilis. It was nearly two years before credible suspicions of foul play emerged. As with so many aspects of this story, there are conflicting accounts of how they came about.

According to Weldon, one day in March 1614 Sir Ralph Winwood, who had finally achieved his ambition of becoming Secretary of State, had occasion to interview the Countess of Shrewsbury, then confined in the Tower for suspected pro-Catholic activities.[7] She told him how Elwes, the Tower Lieutenant, anxious to ingratiate himself with her influential sons-in-law, had revealed to her his suspicions that Overbury had been poisoned. He had not reported them at the time, he said, through fear of the consequences.

This was Weldon's account. Sir Simonds D'Ewes had an altogether different version. According to this, a dinner party was held at the Earl of Shrewsbury's house in the summer of 1615 at which Shrewsbury told Elwes that he wanted to recommend him to Winwood for an office under the Crown. The Secretary had refused on the ground that he could not 'contract friendship with one upon whom did lie a sore suspicion of Overbury's death'. Concerned to remove any impediment to his appointment, Elwes was said to have 'confessed the whole circumstance of the execution of [Overbury's murder] in general, and the instruments to have been set on work by Robert Earl of Somerset and his wife'.

---

[7] The Countess was the aunt of the imprisoned Arbella Stuart.

A New Star Rises

These two accounts of the way in which Overbury's death was for the first time questioned are not necessarily inconsistent one with another. D'Ewes suggests that the dinner party occurred 'by a strange accident', but it could have been the case that the Countess of Shrewsbury's story led to the setting up of the dinner party trap: we simply do not know. In any event, as soon as Winwood judged it prudent to do so he informed the King of what he had been told, possibly at Beaulieu towards the end of the royal progress in September 1615. At first, the King considered the information insufficient to act upon, but this was soon to change. Weldon relates how an apothecary's boy called Reeve, who had prepared some of the poisons, let slip to a servant of William Trumbull, the King's agent in Brussels, how with Elwes' knowledge he had given Overbury a fatal clyster (or enema). Trumbull prudently refused to leave the country lest the boy should abscond, when he would be left as the only source of this explosive information. Arthur Wilson, offered a variant to this story wherein the admission was made on the boy's sickbed, with the additional detail that he had 'died very lately'.[8] If true, this might explain the prosecution's failure to call the boy to give evidence at the trials which followed.

What we can be sure of is that once James was told of these further allegations he immediately gave instructions that the Lieutenant should 'freely set down in writing' what had happened.

ELWES' 'APOLOGY'

Elwes duly presented his written report to the King on 10 September, setting out his version of the circumstances surrounding Overbury's death in what has come to be known as his 'apology'.

---

[8] Arthur Wilson, *The History of Great Britain, Being the Life and Reign of King James I* (Richard Lownds, 1653).

It is a document which deserves to be quoted at length. After the usual obsequious introduction, it read, 'When it pleased your Majesty to make me your own choice for this place [ie the Tower], I found Sir Thomas Overbury a prisoner here. I put a keeper called Weston over him, preferred unto me by Sir Thomas Mounson, (as he and divers others) and with request that he might be a keeper unto Overbury'.

It then went on to outline the occasion described above on which the Lieutenant came across Weston bearing what he assumed to be poisoned broth to the prisoner and berated him for his pains. Elwes went on:

> 'This thing supposed to be given, there was now no more but to hear of the effect. He told them who set him on work, that he had extreme oustings and other tokens, and I intimated as much unto Sir Thomas Mounson, (who, in this business, in my conscience, is as clear as my own soul,) but supposing he might let fall some such word to make the fellow better believed.
>
> This first attempt taking no success, there was advantage taken of my Lord of Somerset's tenderness towards Sir Thomas Overbury, who sent him tarts and potts of jelly. These were counterfeited, and other sent to be presented in their stead, but they were ever prevented; sometimes making his keeper say, my children had desired them; sometimes I made my own cook prepare the like, and in the end, to prevent the pain of continual shifts, his keeper willed the messenger to save labour, seeing he had in the house which pleased him well.
>
> Then bygone your Majesty's progress, by which all such cullerable working was taken away; so as there was no advantage but upon the indisposition of Overbury's body. Here (as God in heaven can witness) I was secure. His physician, Monsr. Mayerne, (who left behind him his directions,) his apothecary, (at the physician's appointment,) an approved honest man as I thought it, and still do.
>
> But (as Weston hath since confessed unto me) here was his overthrow, and that which wrought it was (as he said) a clyster. This apothecary had a servant, who was corrupted. Twenty pounds,

A New Star Rises

Weston said, was given. Who gave it, who corrupted the servant, who told Weston of these things, or what is become of the servant, I can give your Majesty no account; neither can I directly say, that he ever named any as an actor in this business but only Mrs. Turner. If any other were consenting, they two must put the business to a point.

The effect of that which passed between me and Weston the 25th of July last.

It should seem there was lately some whisperings that Sir Thomas Overbury's death would be called in question which came to the ears of some whose conscience must accuse them. Presently a messenger, (being a man of Mr Turner, as Weston said), was sent to Weston, with all speed to meet his mistress at Ware, but, coming thither, found her not. The next day she came as far as Hogston, where, at a tavern, (to use his own words,) they met. There they agreed that if he were examined, he should truly confess who recommended him to me; because in the beginning it was otherwise agreed.

Weston and his mistress were, by appointment, then to meet again at London the 24th July, whither Mrs. Turner came from Grayes. He said he was sent to sound me, whether he could perceive that I had got any inkling of their foresaid foul fact, or no; and if he had, whether he could perceive any desire in me to have it reaved into or not, and what more he could discover in me, for he said they stood doubtful of me. His mistress staid but until his return from me.'

The 'apology' ended with a statement of almost incredible frankness: 'I have set down the truth, peradventure not the whole truth'.

As an explanation from a senior royal official to his Sovereign of the events surrounding the suspected murder of a prisoner in his charge the terms of Elwes' letter beggar belief. He appears to be claiming without explanation that, despite having discovered a plot to kill a royal prisoner, he considered that he had done his duty as the officer in charge simply by admonishing the would-be assassin and allowing him to remain in post, that after becoming aware of further attempts to poison the prisoner he had merely frustrated them by substituting edible for tainted food; and that at no time, then or since, had he considered it his duty to inform the King his master of these appalling goings-on.

Despite this 'apology', Elwes remained at liberty for the time being; instead, James ordered that Richard Weston and Anne Turner should be brought in for questioning, along with the doctor who had attended Overbury and the apothecary. The first to have his collar felt was the gaoler, Weston. In mid-September, after the customary period of solitary confinement designed to soften up suspects, Weston was interrogated by four Privy Councillors and Secretary Winwood. He claimed at first to know of 'no other cause of the suddainnes of [Overbury's] death but the weakness and corrupt indisposition of [his] body'. After further questioning, however, he 'remembered' that on 'going into the Council Chamber in the Tower to see a friend that was in Sir Walter Raleigh's garden, [Overbury] sat so long in a window that he was never well after'. When it was put to Weston that he had 'had a purpose to poison Sir Thomas Overbury' he at first 'utterly denied it', but later admitted that he had been given the glass of 'water' by an apothecary, James Franklin, who lived at the rear of the Exchange (that is the Royal Exchange in the City of London).

Even at this early stage it had become clear that the likely nature and extent of the inquiries were such as to call for the services of a skilled and experienced investigator. Normally this task would have fallen to the Attorney General, Sir Francis Bacon, but the King decided to entrust it instead to his great rival, the sixty-three-year-old Sir Edward Coke, the Lord Chief Justice.[9]

---

[9] Coke was in fact Chief Justice of the Court of King's Bench, a post which was then known informally as that of Lord Chief Justice.

THE INVESTIGATION BEGINS

The tall, obsessive Coke was one of England's foremost jurists. He had collected the first reputable series of law reports and was later to write his magisterial *Institutes of the Laws of England*. Coke had for years incurred James' disapproval, even wrath, by defending the common law against royal privilege, but it was his relentlessly bullying prosecution of Sir Walter Raleigh which had given him the reputation of the most effective and feared prosecutor in the land, which was no doubt the reason behind James' decision to appoint him to conduct the investigation. Coke's undoubted abilities were unfortunately counterbalanced by a serious lack of prudence and restraint, coupled with a susceptibility to conspiracy theories. The proceedings which followed his investigations were to give full rein to both weaknesses.

Coke began work on 27 September by resuming the examination of Richard Weston; and for the first time the truth began to come out. After retracting his earlier story that it was Franklin who had given him the 'water' for Overbury Weston admitted that it had in fact come from Frances, Countess of Essex, via his son who was then in her service. He had met the Countess at the prompting of Mrs Turner and was told that he would be well rewarded for his pains. The water would do the prisoner no harm, she said, but he himself should not drink it. He drew the obvious conclusion.

Weston went on to confirm in substance Elwes' account of the occasion when the Lieutenant had come across him while he was on his way to Overbury bearing the prisoner's soup and the 'water', and of how he had been castigated for his pains. The following day, he said, he had thrown the glass into the gutter, breaking it, but had lied about this to Mrs Turner, pretending that he had followed her instructions and that the liquid, had made Overbury very sick ('extreme oustings', as Elwes graphically described it). Two or three weeks later he was contacted by Franklin and the two men arranged to meet in a tavern. When asked how Overbury was getting on, Weston replied that he was not well and was receiving 'much physick and many clysters'. Franklin then told him that someone other than the prisoner's normal apothecary had been given £20 to administer a clyster to the prisoner.

The following day Weston revealed how on one occasion the Countess had sent him a 'little pot of white jelly'. Fearing that it was poison, he had 'cast it into a homely place'. He did the same with some tarts which she had sent in. Notwithstanding this, Overbury had become sick about a month before he died 'and decayed much in that sickeness'. After his death Weston was rewarded by the Countess with a 'gift' of one hundred pounds for his services. At his final interrogation on 6 October, Weston added that two or three days before his death Overbury had been given a clyster by Paul de Loubell. The clyster, he said, was not responsible for the plasters which were found on the dead man's body; they had been applied by Sir Thomas' own servant, Lawrence Davies, to treat 'an issue (discharge) on the left side of his head and on his back and on his left foot'.

When Davies was questioned in his turn he revealed that Carr had sent a letter to Overbury, probably on 9 June, which contained a white powder. It was enough to galvanize the chief justice into immediate action.

THE LOVERS' LAST MEETING

So urgent did Coke consider his news to be that on 11 October he rode all night from London to the royal hunting lodge at Royston in Hertfordshire where the King was staying at the start of his winter journey. James seems to have been genuinely shocked to learn that his former lover was suspected of having been involved in Overbury's death. 'They have made me a pimp to carry on their bawdry and murder', he exclaimed. Realizing that he was now

A New Star Rises

moving into the most difficult and delicate territory, Coke asked for additional support in his investigations. Three commissioners were duly appointed for the purpose. They were the Duke of Lennox, Lord Chancellor Ellesmere and Lord Zouch. It was a well-balanced team; Lennox was a friend of Carr's, Ellesmere was quite the opposite, and Zouch was a man with a foot in neither camp.

Somehow learning what had happened and aghast at Ellesmere's appointment, Carr rushed post-haste to Royston to reverse it – on horseback rather than in the customary coach. But James would not change his mind and the dejected Earl prepared to leave for London. Weldon paints a vivid picture of their parting:

> 'The Earl when he kissed his hand, the King hung about his neck, slabboring his cheeks; saying, "for Gods sake, when shall I see thee again; On my soul, I shall neither eat nor sleep until you come again"; the Earl told him, "on Monday (this being on the Friday,) for Gods sake let me" said the King, "shall I, shall I?" Then lolled about his neck; then, "for Gods sake, give thy lady this kiss for me"; in the same manner at the stayres head, at the middle of the stayres, and at the stayres foot; the Earl was not in his coach, when the King used these very words (in the hearing of four Servants, of whom one was Somerset's great creature, and of the Bed-chamber, who reported it instantly to the Author of this History) "I shall never see his face more."'

Roger Coke's account is altogether less favourable to James:

> 'The King had a loathsome way of lolling his arms about his Favourites' necks, and kissing them; and in this posture the messenger found the King with Somerset, saying: "When shall I see thee again?" Somerset then designing for London, when he was arrested by Sir Edward's warrant. Somerset exclaimed, that never such an affront was offered to a Peer of England in the presence of the King. "Nay man," said the King, "if Coke sends for me, I must

go too;" and when he was gone, "Now the De'el go with thee, said the King, for I will never see thy face any more."'[10]

Some have read this latter account as evidence of James' cynical attitude towards his former lover, but nothing in Weldon's book supports this and such disloyalty to a former lover would in any event be contrary to the King's known character. To the end of his days, James seems never to have deserted a friend: quite the reverse, he was overly indulgent towards them, even when they did not deserve it.

The face-to-face meeting having failed to move the King, Carr wrote to him in a renewed attempt to have Ellesmere removed from the investigation, but he went too far when he threatened that if James persisted in countenancing his accusers he would lose the support of the whole house of Howard. James wrote back indignantly refusing the request. Carr, he complained, had 'bestowed so much scribbling and railing, covertly against me and avowedly against the chancellor'. Ever since the beginning of this business, James went on, 'both your father-in-law and ye have ever and at all times behaved yourselves quite contrary to the form that men that wish the trial of the verity ever did in such a case'. The letter ended by declaring:

> 'If the delation [accusation] prove false, God so deal with my soul as no man among you shall so much rejoice at it as I; nor shall ever spare, I vow to God, one grain of rigour that can be stretched against the conspirators. If otherwise (as God forbid) none of you shall more heartily sorrow for it; and never King used that clemency as I will do in such a case. But that I should suffer a murder (if it be so) to be suppressed and plastered over to the destruction of both my soul and reputation, I am no Christian. Fail not to show this letter to your father-in-law [James concluded] and that both of you read it twice over'.

---

[10] Roger Coke, *Detection of the Court and State of England* (J. Brotherton & W. Meadows, 1696).

The purport of the King's letter was clear: even their friendship would not be allowed to stand in the way of justice: Carr could no longer be in doubt of his position.

Weldon tells an interesting story of James. He gives it no date, but it appears to have taken place at about this time. The King is said to have summoned his judges, knelt before them and made this solemn declaration:

> 'My Lords the Judges, it is lately come to my hearing that you have now in examination a business of poisoning. Lord! in what a miserable condition shall this Kingdom be (the only famous nation for hospitality in the world) if our tables should become such a snare, as that none could eat without danger of life, and that Italian custom should be introduced among us! Therefore, my Lords, I charge you, as you will answer it at that great and dreadful day of judgment, that you examine it strictly, without favour, affection, or partiality. And if you shall spare any guilty of this crime, God's curse light on you and your posterity! and if I spare any that are guilty, God's curse light on me and my posterity for ever!'

He was to have cause to regret these words later.

CARR COVERS HIS TRACKS

Now the subject of an investigation for murder, Carr wrote to Winwood complaining of his having brought the matter to the King's attention and reminding the Secretary to whom he owed his post. Winwood answered curtly that he could not conceal what he knew for the safety of his life and conscience, and reminded the Earl that he had paid £7,000 for his office.

Frustrated at every turn, Carr began desperately trying to cover his tracks. First, he sent his servant, Rawlins, to demand from Overbury's former servant, Davies, the return of the letters which had passed between their two masters. But Davies was a man with a grievance. When Overbury died Carr had promised him a job which had not materialized. Accordingly, while Davies handed over some thirty-odd letters, he kept back two or three. Realizing that they were missing, Carr renewed his request, bolstering it with a gift of £30 and hinting that a job would also be forthcoming. Davies agreed to produce the remaining letters; but, like the Earl, never lived up to his promise.

Carr next turned for help to a good friend who happened to have been the administrator of Northampton's estate. Sir Robert Cotton was a courtier who, like so many others, had been knighted by James in recognition of his support in obtaining the English throne. He was a noted antiquarian who possessed one of the best libraries in the land. Though not a lawyer, he was often consulted on legal matters. At Carr's request, Cotton handed over some thirty of his letters to Northampton, most of which Carr promptly burned. The rest, consisting largely of letters he had received from Northampton and Overbury, were returned to Cotton for safe-keeping. Carr was later to admit having edited some of those he retained 'as impertinent' (that is, irrelevant) and to having asked Cotton to edit and add dates to others. Eyebrows were raised later when it was realized that the effect of the alterations was to suggest that Overbury was still in good health long after the poisons were said to have been administered.

The day that he burned the letters (16 October) Carr took an even more desperate step: he issued a warrant to break into the lodgings of Richard Weston's son and seize any letters which were found there belonging to Mrs Turner. The warrant was executed and a trunk full of documents handed over to the Earl; what became of it no one knows. Although Carr was to claim to have issued the warrant in his capacity as a Privy Councillor, he must have known that the act was well beyond his powers. As we shall see, it was to lead to disastrous consequences for him.

A search of Anne Turner's house revealed a positive pharmacopoeia of poisons which seemed to lend substance to

Weston's story. They included realgar, aqua fortis, white arsenic, corrosive sublimate, diamond powder, lapis causticus, something described as 'great spider' and cantharides. Since some of these substances were to figure prominently in the trials which followed it may be helpful to consider just what they were and how they would affect anyone to whom they were administered.

THE POISONS

White arsenic, or arsenic trioxide, when dissolved in water is an odourless and colourless substance. Widely used to kill rats, arsenic was readily available and easy to administer. (It was not for nothing that it became known as 'inheritance powder'.) When eaten, arsenic can cause fever, vomiting, abdominal pains, kidney damage, bloody diarrhoea and, of course, death. At lower doses it produces anaemia, loss of hair and characteristic white lines (the Mees stripes) on the fingernails. White arsenic is to be distinguished from rosalgar (red arsenic or realgar), old names for arsenic sulphide, a common ingredient of fireworks.

According to Dr John Emsley, a recent medical writer, the first symptom of a fatal dose of arsenic can occur in an ordinary person between fifteen minutes to many hours after administration, depending on the amount of food in the stomach. Vomiting starts too late to remove the arsenic that has been absorbed into the system, although it may expel the remainder of a massive dose before it has time to be digested. The victim may complain of thirst and a sore mouth and throat, and experience difficulty in swallowing. Drink does not assuage the thirst and the stomach becomes painful and sensitive to pressure. Diarrhoea begins after about twelve hours. In acute cases the pulse is weak and rapid and the skin cold, damp and pale. Death occurs within twelve to thirty-six hours, but some patients have been known to linger for four days.[11]

Aqua fortis, or nitric acid, is a corrosive which, if drunk, will burn the mouth and gullet and can cause hypotension (low blood pressure) and death by acute kidney failure. In Overbury's day, diamond powder was assumed to be toxic. In fact, if eaten, it would probably be harmless, though large fragments might cause intestinal bleeding. Lapis causticus, or potassium hydroxide, is a strong alkaline corrosive in the form of a white or yellow solid or powder which is soluble in water. If ingested, it can burn the mouth and throat, cause difficulty swallowing, and bring about vomiting and abdominal pain. Cantharides, or Spanish fly, is a yellow/brown powder derived from a dried beetle, *Lytta vesicatoria*. Apart from its well-known priapic effect (it was an early form of Viagra), cantharides can cause burning thirst, bad breath, gastro-intestinal irritation, vomiting, bloody stools, suppression of urine, convulsions and kidney damage, sometimes even death.

Goodness knows what 'great spider' was.

Despite the discovery of all these noxious substances in her house Anne Turner, when arrested, brazenly denied everything. Elwes, who for the time being had been allowed his liberty, continued to stick by the story he had told the King. But when the Commissioners came to interview James Franklin they must have thought they had discovered the pot of gold.

FRANKLIN'S TALES

Some of the most outrageous allegations which emerged in the Overbury investigations were to come from James Franklin, who called himself 'doctor', but who in fact had nothing in the way of

---

[11] Dr John Emsley, *The Elements of Murder: A History of Poison* (Oxford, Oxford University Press, 2005).

medical qualifications. According to Sir Simonds D'Ewes, Franklin was 'a man of a reasonable stature, crook-shouldered, of a swarthy complexion, and thought to be no less a wizard than ... Gresham and Forman'. His red-bearded face, disfigured by venereal disease, did little to dispel the impression of infamy which surrounded someone who claimed to be able to raise the dead and was suspected of having poisoned his first wife. Along with all his other unprepossessing qualities, Franklin was an habitual liar. It is hard to know why the authorities were prepared to give him the credence they did. It could only be that, as someone privy to the conspiracy, enough of his story was based on fact to give a colouring of truth to the rest.

Franklin made a written statement on 16 November which, like all the others he made, has not survived. Coke was to summarize it at Elwes trial as follows:

'Mrs. Turner came to me from the Countess [Frances], and wished me from her to get the strongest poison I could for sir T. Overbury. Accordingly I bought seven, viz. aqua fortis, white arsenick, mercury, powder of diamonds, lapis costitus, great spiders, and cantharides: All these were given to sir T. Overbury at several times. And further confesseth, that the Lieutenant knew of these poisons; for that appeared, said he, by many letters which he writ to the Countess of Essex, which I saw, and thereby knew that he knew of this matter; One of these letters I read for the Countess, because she could not read it herself in which the Lieutenant used this speech; "Madam, the scab is like the fox, the more he is cursed, the better he fareth"; and many other speeches. Sir T. never eat white salt, but there was white arsenick put into it: once he desired pig, and Mrs. Turner put into it lapis costitus. The white powder that was sent to Sir T. in a letter he knew to be white arsenick.

At another time he had two partridges sent him from the court; and water and onions being the sauce, Mrs. Turner put in cantharides instead of pepper; so that there was scarce any thing that he did eat, but there was some poison mixed. For these poisons the Countess sent me rewards: She sent many times gold by Mrs. Turner. She afterwards wrote unto me to buy her more poisons. I went unto her, and told her I was weary of it; and I besought her upon my knees, that she would use me no more in those matters: But she importuned me, bad me go, and enticed me with fair speeches and rewards; so she overcame me, and did bewitch me.

The cause of this poisoning, as the Countess told him, was because Sir T. Overbury would pry so far into their suit as he would put them down. He did also say that the toothless maid, trusty Margaret, was acquainted with the poisoning; so was Mrs. Turner's man Stephen;[12] so also Mrs. Horne, the Countess's own hand-maid. He saith, On the marriage-day of the Countess with Somerset [Carr] she sent him £20. by Mrs. Turner; and he was to have been paid by the Countess £200. per annum during his life. That he was urged and haunted two hundred several times, at least, by the Countess to do it against his conscience. He saith, she was able to bewitch any man; and then he wrought the love between Rochester [Carr] and her; and that he had 12 several letters from her to prosecute it, and was to have to continue their loves until the marriage; and that all things were burnt since the first discovery.'

There is much about this 'confession' which is simply incredible. Franklin's statement that Frances could not read, for example, was manifestly untrue because letters in her handwriting were produced to the court. The promise of a reward of £200 a year for life too is highly questionable, representing as it does an improbably large reward in those days, even for murder.

By now Coke had carried out and meticulously recorded nearly three hundred examinations.[13] Professor Amos, who studied all the evidence deposited in the State Paper Office, concluded that

---

[12] Stephen Clapham was Frances' groom of the chamber.
[13] Not all were grim; consider the delightful story of, 'one Symon, a servant of Sir Thomas Monson, who was imployed in carrying jelly and tart to the Tower; who, upon his examination, for his pleasant answer was instantly dismissed. My lord told him, "Symon, you have a hand in this poysoning business." — "No, my good lord, I had but one finger in it, which almost cost me my life, and at the best, cost me all my hair and nails;" for the truth was, Symon was somewhat liquorish, and finding the sirrup swim from the top of a tart as he carryed, he did with his finger skim it off; and it was to be believed, had he known what it had been, he would not have been his taster at so dear a rate'.

A New Star Rises

'they indicate patient industry and a zeal for accumulating proof which disclaimed no mental drudgery nor even manual labour'.[14] Even Coke's great rival, Bacon, was moved to concede that 'never man's person and his place were better met in a business, than my lord Coke and my Lord Chief Justice, in the case of Overbury'.[15] When it came to producing the fruits of his investigations in court, however, Coke was to fall below these high standards.

But before the trials could begin a tactical decision had first to be made.

---

[14] Andrew Amos, *The Great Oyer of Poisoning: The Trial of the Earl of Somerset for the possible poisoning of Sir Thomas Overbury* (London, Richard Bentley, 1846), p. 363.

[15] Francis Bacon, *Declaration of the Treason of Robert, Earl of Essex* (printed by F. Bacon.).

ACT 7

'A NET TO CATCH LITTLE FISHES'

Before the lesser parties could be prosecuted the principal offender, what the law calls the principal in the first degree, had first to be brought to justice, but who was this to be? The apothecary who was thought to have administered the 'fatal enema' had strong claims to the title, but, if he ever did exist, he was not charged with the crime or even offered as a witness, possibly because he was already dead. That only left the man who had confessed to being a party to the poisoning. And so it was that on 19 October 1615, Richard Weston came to stand his trial before a crowded court at London's ancient Guildhall.[1] On the bench were Lord Mayor Hayes, Lord Chief Justice Coke, Justices Dodderidge and Haughton, Serjeant (Sir Randolph) Crewe and the Recorder of London, Sir Henry Montague, each of whom had been appointed for the occasion as special Commissioners of oyer and terminer,[2] as the judges of the superior criminal courts were known.[3]

---

[1] Except where otherwise stated, all accounts of the Overbury trials are taken from *Howells' State Trials* collection, the reliability of which is considered below.
[2] 'To hear and determine'.
[3] A Serjeant was a rank of senior counsel.

WESTON ON TRIAL

As the law stood in those days allegations of the most serious offences had to be heard in the first instance before what was called a grand jury of fourteen men who would decide whether the indictment, or formal charge, amounted to *billa vera,* or true bill, that is to say, an accusation which justified a trial.[4] In his opening address to the jury, Coke urged them to show by their verdict 'the baseness of poisoning above all other kinds of murder'. Few offences, he said, were more serious. The statute of Henry VIII which had made poisoning a treasonable offence gruesomely recited how in 1531 Richard Roose, a cook in the household of the Bishop of Rochester, had been attainted for poisoning a batch of gruel resulting in the deaths of two people. His fate was to be boiled alive at Smithfield. By Carr's time, poisoning had been downgraded to a felony punishable by hanging, but it was a crime which was still regarded with disgust. After an hour's retirement to consider the evidence, the grand jury returned and sent the case for trial. They were promptly ushered out of court, to be replaced by a petty, or trial, jury of twelve men. Strange as it may appear to modern eyes, Coke the investigator was now translated into Coke the judge.

Weston's trial got off to a rocky start. When the charge was put to him he could do nothing but repeat, 'Lord have mercy on me. Lord have mercy on me'. After some time he timorously pleaded not guilty, but immediately threw everything into confusion by refusing to consent to trial by jury, saying only that he would be tried by God. It should be explained that in those days for a trial to begin the defendant had to agree to trial by jury, as opposed to other forms of trial, such as trial by combat, despite the fact that

---

[4] Grand juries, though long gone from England, still flourish in America.

Passion, Poison and Power

they had long fallen into disuse.[5] Had nothing further been done, therefore, Weston's refusal would in Bacon's words, have 'arrested the wheel of justice'.

Coke had been warned privately in advance that the prisoner had been put up to this stratagem by Sir Henry Yelverton, the Solicitor General and a friend of the Howards, in order to prevent the prosecution of the Somersets. Furious that his carefully laid plans were on the point of being frustrated, the Chief Justice took an hour to spell out in detail to Weston the consequences which would ensue if he should persist in refusing trial by jury, notably the dreadful *forte peine et dure*.[6] It did no good: Weston stuck to his guns.

But it was what Coke did next which startled everyone. He directed Lawrence Hyde, the Queen's Attorney and nominal prosecutor, to outline in open court the evidence against the accused. So far, so good, but Coke went on to instruct that 'if in the declaration thereof they may meet with any great persons whatsoever, as certainly there were great ones confederate in that fact, he should boldly and faithfully open whatsoever was necessary, and he could prove against them'. It was the clearest direction, seemingly prearranged, that Hyde should publicly reveal the supposed role of Carr and Frances in Overbury's murder.

When Hyde rose to his feet, therefore, he dramatically accused the Earl and Countess of Somerset of being the 'principal movers' in the plot to murder Overbury. She in particular, he suggested,

---

[5] Trial by combat was last claimed (though not carried out) in a case of 1818.

[6] The *forte peine et dure* involved weights being placed on the naked prisoner and increased little by little until his death. Some had been known to withstand this torment for eight or nine days. During this time they were allowed only the coarsest bread to eat or, on alternate days, water from the nearest puddle to drink.

was a 'dead and rotten branch' whose family would prosper better if she were removed. (Later, after Frances had agreed to cooperate, the prosecution were to paint an entirely more flattering picture of her.) The plot, said Hyde, had been conceived as a means of smoothing the path of Frances' annulment by getting rid of Overbury, 'whose worth and valour were not unknown to the King'. (Once again, it was a characterization that was to be turned on its head when it became convenient to the prosecution to do so.) After describing how Carr had persuaded Sir Thomas to refuse the post of ambassador, Hyde went on to outline the roles the minor characters had played in the poisoning.

The public, in court and out, realized at once the injustice of what had taken place: the Earl and his wife had been publicly condemned of a crime for which they had not even been indicted. Coke got to hear the rumbles of their disapproval and, after pondering overnight on what he had done, was moved to concede from the Bench that there had been 'certain criticks, who had ... found much fault' with his direction. He sought to justify himself by claiming that it was 'exceedingly discreet and convenient that the world should receive some satisfaction in a cause of this nature ... notwithstanding the greatness of any who might thereby be impeached'. But these bold words were merely a smokescreen; the general view, then, as now, was that Coke had quite consciously taken the opportunity to blacken Frances' and Robert's names before they had had a chance to defend themselves, a blatant abuse of his powers as a judge.

During the four-day adjournment given to allow Weston to reflect on his dilemma, the bishops of London and Ely visited him in his cell to urge him to go along with the proceedings (presumably, we must hope, for the sake of his soul). This did the trick and when the prisoner was brought back to court he meekly consented to be tried, in the words of the old rubric, 'by God and my country'. In Coke's written report to the King (though not in *The State Trials*)

Weston is quoted as adding this telling qualification to his assent: 'But I hope that they will not make a net to catch the little fishes as flies and let the great go'. He was to use the very same words again after his conviction, but his wish was not to be fulfilled.

As we shall see, the indictment when it was read out was quite specific as to what poisons had been administered to Overbury and on which dates, although it did not specify which poison was believed to have killed the prisoner. The Chief Justice explained why: '[A]lbeit the poisoning ... be said to be with Rosalgar, White Arsenick, and Mercury Sublimate, yet the Jury were not to expect precise proof in that point, shewing how impossible it were to convict a poisoner who useth not to take any witnesses to the composing of his sibber sauces'.[1] It was a fair point: the rough and ready science of the day simply could not say with certainty what poison had been administered to a dead man, or when; still less, it should be added, could it discover whether the poison was the cause of death.

It fell to Lawrence Hyde to describe to the jury how the plot had worked. Weston, he said, had been 'preferred', that is to say recommended, to the post of under-keeper 'by Mrs. Turner upon the means and request of Sir T. Monson'. He had been told that 'if he gave Sir T. Overbury [that] which the Countess would send him he should be well rewarded'. Weston's son had brought him 'a glass of water of a yellowish and greenish colour' which the Countess had given him, along with a warning not to drink it.[2] Naturally suspecting that it contained poison, Weston had put the glass aside in 'a little study', but told Mrs. Turner that he had in fact

---

[1] As applied to the condiments of the table, 'sipper sauces means those extra ingredients or compounds which give a zest to the food'. *Notes and Queries,* 25 June 1964.
[2] *The Harleian Miscellany* (London, Robert Dutton, 1810) described it as a 'glass of blue water'.

given it to Overbury, 'and demanded his reward'. She replied that he would have none of it until Overbury was dead. Finally, Hyde asserted that on 14 September 1613, Weston 'and the apothecary [still unnamed] ministered the clyster to Sir T which gave him sixty stools and vomits, and that he died the next day'. About a year after Overbury's death, Weston was said to have received £180 from Mrs Turner, while the apothecary got £20. Finally, the prosecution read out the testimony of various witnesses, as well as Elwes' 'apology' and several letters.

Asked what he had to say for himself, Weston seemed perplexed. He confessed to having 'received the said glass, and thought it was not good', but continued to deny having given it to the prisoner. Asked why he had tried to lay the blame on Franklin, 'he confessed it was to save his child'. In the end he could, in the words of *The State Trials*, 'say nothing that had any colour of material or substantial point to excuse or argue any innocency in him'. It did not take the jury long to find him guilty, after which the court pronounced the inevitable sentence of death by hanging. It was carried out two days later at what was known as Tyburn Tree, near the site of the present Marble Arch and the traditional place of execution. The event did not pass without incident.

Among the crowd of spectators at the gallows was Overbury's brother-in-law, Sir John Lidcote, and a number of Overbury's friends, among them Sir John Wentworth and Sir John Holles (later first Earl of Clare). As the rope was being put around the prisoner's neck they pushed their horses through the throng, Wentworth dramatically calling out to the condemned man, 'I ask you. Did you poison Sir Thomas Overbury?'. Ignoring the question, Weston turned to the sheriff and pitiably muttered, 'You promised I should not be troubled at this time'. Before being swung off into eternity he declared, 'I die not unworthily', adding enigmatically, 'My Lord Chief Justice hath my mind under his hand, and he is an honourable judge'. Wentworth and his friends were later fined and imprisoned for their conduct, but Lidcote escaped prosecution in return for giving evidence against the rest.

Weston had made a bad showing in court, but in fact the evidence against him had been thin in the extreme, to modern eyes at least: some tarts that he had brought into the Tower had turned black, but there was no proof that they or the 'water' he had been caught taking to Overbury were in fact poisoned, no proof that the tarts or the liquid were ever consumed by their intended victim, and no proof that they were the cause of his death. Bacon, were he still alive, would no doubt point out, as he did at the trial, that the toxicology of his day did not allow such detail, but this is an insufficient excuse when the only evidence was that the substances had never actually reached their intended victim. The jury were not told of Weston's assertion that he had thrown away the 'water' or of the Lieutenant's claim to have substituted edible tarts for the poisoned ones. Nor did the prosecution give any explanation why they had not called the apothecary to give evidence. In the face of Weston's plea of not guilty, no jury today could possibly have convicted him of murder – and no jury then should have.

Three days after the gaoler's conviction Elwes was dismissed as Lieutenant of the Tower and placed under house arrest, but he was not the next to be tried.

'A SPEEDY AND ORDINARY TRIAL'

With Weston safely convicted and in his grave, the way was clear to prosecute the first of the accessories.

While awaiting trial, Anne Turner had been held under house arrest at the home of an Alderman. There she had been visited by Carr who had assured her that she would be free in two or three days. Frances wrote to her with a similar assurance, enclosing with her letter a gift of a diamond ring and a diamond cross. (The

Alderman's wife, too, received a gift for her kind usage of her charge.) The feisty Anne had consistently denied the 'malicious and scandalous' accusations made against her. A fortnight after her arrest she petitioned the Lord Chief Justice indignantly demanding either to be brought to 'a speedy and ordinary trial' or to be released. To her dismay, Coke chose the former, and on 7 November 1615 she appeared before the Court of King's Bench in Westminster Hall. (The location of each trial depended upon where the crime was alleged to have been committed.) She was charged with the same offences as Weston, but also with 'comforting and aiding' him in committing them.

Anne was dressed in her best finery, complete with ruff and cuffs dyed in her signature yellow and wearing a fine hat, which immediately attracted Coke's displeasure, 'You are not in church now, madame, but must be uncovered'. The hat came off, to be replaced by a handkerchief. It was a small matter, but it seems to have unsettled Anne. Laurence Hyde opened for the prosecution by describing to the jury the close relationship between Frances, Weston and Forman, whom he described as a sinister practitioner of the black arts. And not without justification: when the doctor's house had been searched a quantity of incriminating items was found, among them a parchment with a piece of human skin attached to it. Documents were produced bearing magic spells and 'the Devil's particular names, who were conjured to torment the Lord Somerset [Carr] and [Anne's lover] Sir Arthur Mainwaring, if their loves should not continue, the one to the Countess, the other to Mrs. Turner'. The two women's purpose, claimed Hyde, was 'by force of magic [to] procure the now Earl of Somerset, then Viscount Rochester, to love her, and Sir Arthur Manwaring (sic) to love Mrs. Turner'.

It was during the production of these strange artifacts that the supernatural made its presence felt. When Hyde produced a lead figurine of a copulating couple which had been found in the

Passion, Poison and Power

magician's house, a great crack was heard in the scaffolding on which the spectators were seated. It took the tipstaffs a quarter of an hour to quell their superstitious fears.[3]

Probably the most embarrassing item found in Mrs. Turner's possession was Forman's list of ladies of the court, which was said to include the names of their respective lovers. According to one source, 'The Lord Chief Justice Coke grasped this startling document, glanced his eye over it, and then insisted it should not be read'.[4] Weldon repeated a common scandal when he observed that this was because 'the first leafe my Lord Cook lighted on he found his owne wive's name'. If true, this might explain why the official report did not tell the full story.

When Coke came to give what is called the judge's charge to the jury (that is, his instructions on how to go about their duties), he took the opportunity once again to defame the absent Earl:

> '... what a great vexation and grief it was to the King, that Somerset [Carr] only by making use of his favour and love, so foul a fact was done; as, 1st, To be the occasion to put sir T. Overbury to employment for the embassage at Russia; and 2dly, to make him refuse the same, and to give right cause for his commitment: 3dly, To bear him in hand, that he would work his liberty, but still aggravated and laboured the contrary, and gave directions to the Lieutenant of the Tower, to look surely to him, and to keep him close prisoner, and that he should send to none of his friends, or they to him, urging great matters against him.'

Coke then turned his full venom on the prisoner, condemning her for seven deadly sins: 'for she was a whore, a bawd, a sorcerer, a witch, a papist, a felon and a murderess'. It was hardly the

---

[3] Thomas Wright, *Narratives of Sorcery and Magic* (Detroit, Gale Research Co., 1851).
[4] William Goodman, *The Social History of Great Britain During the Reigns of the Stuarts* (New York, William H. Colyer, 1844).

language to be expected of a judge towards someone who had not yet been found guilty.

In her distress, Anne could only think to ask the court for mercy; she had, she said, ever been brought up with the Countess and had become her servant, and she was unaware that the food sent to the Tower contained poison. It did her no good, for after a short retirement the jury returned to court to announce their verdict of guilty. Anne was rendered speechless by weeping and was unable to respond to the customary invitation to say why sentence should not be passed upon her. After the dreadful words had been pronounced, Mr Justice Crook intervened to confide to the prisoner his belief that she had had a very honourable trial by men such as he had not seen for one of her (low) rank and quality. It is doubtful whether the poor woman took much comfort from this assurance.

The general view at the time was that the normally self-confident Anne had failed to give a good account of herself at her trial. One reason for this may have been that it was only during those proceedings that she had learned for the first time in court of Weston's conviction and execution, which knowledge 'so much dejected her that in a manner she spake nothing for herself'.

The day after her conviction, Anne was visited in her cell by an Anglican minister who sought to prepare her for the next world. As a Roman Catholic, she objected to making her confession to someone she believed did not have the power to take it. In the end, however, she consented to be shriven, and later professed to die a Protestant. According to the minister, she admitted to having been a 'most vile, abominable and monstrous sinner'. She said that, although she did not want to 'hurt that lady that formed the plot, for she was as dear to me as my own soul', she had indeed known of Frances' plan to kill Overbury and had done nothing about it. 'Franklin', she added bitterly, 'is a villain', and she pleaded not to be hanged on the same day as him.

Anne's confession that she knew of the plot but took no active part in it was only a half-truth: there is ample evidence that she knowingly helped in the procurement of the poisons. But who can blame a condemned woman for seeking whatever small comfort she could from minimizing her guilt? In any event, she made a good death, distributing money to the crowd from the cart taking her to the scaffold. In her last moments she asked the onlookers to take example from her fate, declaring that, 'When her hand was once in this business she knew the revealing of it would be her overthrow'. She asked for and was given permission to pray for Frances. After calling on God to protect her children, she knelt and said the Lord's prayer. Her hands were tied with a black ribbon, her head was covered in a black veil and the cart was driven away from under her. It was a cruel death far removed from judicial hanging as practised in the twentieth century, but these were cruel times and she had, after all, tried repeatedly to procure the death of another.

As was so often the case with pretty young women, Anne's sorry fate evoked much popular sympathy, but the fashion for yellow ruffs died with her.[5]

'MY LORD, YOU HAVE NOT OBSERVED YOUR RULE'

Now it was Elwes' turn in the dock. Just over a week after Anne had gone to her fate, the former Lieutenant of the Tower was

---

[5] There is no truth, wrote Judge E.A. Parry, in the old story that Coke ordered her to be executed in the yellow ruff she had made the fashion and so proudly worn in Court. What did happen, according to Sir Simonds D'Ewes, was that the hangman, a coarse ruffian with a distorted sense of humour, dressed himself in bands and cuffs of yellow colour, but no one heeded his ribaldry; only in after days none of either sex used the yellow starch, and the fashion grew generally to be detested (Parry, *The Overbury Mystery* (London, Fisher Unwin, 1925)).

'A Net to Catch Little Fishes'

brought to the Guildhall to be tried for the 'malicious aiding, comforting, and abetting of Weston in the poisoning and murdering of Overbury'. At the very start of the trial, Coke made a dramatic announcement, grandiloquently informing the jury that, 'You my masters, shall hear strange and stupendous things, such as the ears of men never heard of'. Apparently, he had got it into his head that Overbury's death was part of some vast Rome-inspired conspiracy which threatened whole swathes of society, not stopping short of the throne. It was a theme to which he was to return more than once.

Coke's fantasies aside, the report in *The State Trials* gives little detail of the case against Elwes, apart from extracts from two letters from Northampton to Rochester and Elwes' letter to Carr reporting on his attempts to 'turn' Overbury in the matter of the annulment. The court was also told of a letter from the Countess which asked him to give some tarts to the prisoner 'for there were letters in them'.

Overbury's father had once described Elwes as 'a dexterous and witty man' – indeed, he had been a contemporary of his son's at the Middle Temple – and the former Lieutenant was not going to give in without a fight. He began boldly by reminding the Chief Justice of how he had often heard him express pity for the state of an unrepresented defendant faced with a capable prosecuting advocate, fearful for his life and his wife and family. 'You have protested that you had rather hang in hell than for mercy to such a one, than for judgement. My lord', he went on, 'you have not observed your rule in my cause'. Coke did not rise to the bait and Elwes had, like all the others, to present his defence without benefit of legal representation.

Elwes now offered for the first time an explanation for his strange reaction when he met Weston bearing the 'poisoned glass'. The gaoler's question to him, he said, had not been 'Shall I give him this now?', but 'Shall I give him it now?'. His point was that

109

Passion, Poison and Power

he believed Weston to be referring, not to any glass in the gaoler's hand, but merely to the broth he was carrying. In response, he said, he had:

> '[beaten Weston] down and reproved him with God's judgement; nay, I humbled him so that upon his knees he thanked God and me and told me that he and his had cause to bless God for me and that I withheld him from doing that act; and if you call this comforting and abetting, to terrify a man for his sins, and to make him to confess his fault to God; and so abhor and detest the act then was I an abettor and comforter to Weston.'

Elwes seemed to consider it a point in his favour that when the tarts that Frances had sent in for Overbury went black and bad in his kitchen he had merely had them thrown away and others prepared in their place.

The accused did what he could to distance himself from Weston. He had accepted the man as Overbury's keeper on the recommendation of Northampton and Monson, 'whom I took to be my friends and thought they would commend no man to be keeper which might in any way endanger me'. He sought to explain away Northampton's written instructions by saying that they referred, not to poisoning, but to his efforts to win Overbury round to the idea of the proposed marriage. As for the letters from the Countess, he never understood them in anything 'but the[ir] bare literal meaning'. However, his confidence was shaken when he was asked what he had meant when he had written, 'Rochester's part I shall greatly fear until I see the event to be clearly carried'. At this, the report says, Elwes 'staggered and wavered much' and gave no convincing explanation of the words.

But he soon recovered his composure and argued, somewhat ingenuously, that he could not be guilty because he had made 'a free and voluntary discovery of [the plot] myself' – ignoring entirely the fact that he had done so years after the event and only when his involvement had already come to light. He also claimed merit for having incriminated the 'real' poisoner, Weston. 'Here I am indicted as accessory before the fact when I knew nothing until after the fact'. Even more curiously, he sought to blacken the name of Thomas Howard, Frances' father, 'If I be in the plot', he said, 'the lord treasurer [Suffolk] is, I have his letter to shew in it: he called me to his lodging, and said, "The plots you know them as well as I, the plots were only to repair her honour"'; 'my wife', he went on, 'hath the letters from my lord treasurer and Monson; for these plots I will run willingly to my death, if circumstances be knit with any manner of fact'. It is quite possible that Suffolk was involved in the plot to imprison and 'turn' Overbury, but Elwes seems to have been suggesting more when he spoke of the Lord Treasurer being involved in 'plots', plural. It is a curious word which may never be explained, always assuming, of course, the text to be accurate on this point.

After telling the court that he was guilty of nothing worse than ill judgement, Elwes posed a hypothetical question, 'If one knoweth not of any plot to poison a man but only suspecteth, is no actor or contriver himself, only imagineth such a thing. Whether such a one can be accessory to the murder?'. 'Concealing without malice', he suggested, 'could not be abetting'. It was a good lawyer's point which deserved an answer, but Coke ignored it altogether. Instead, the Chief Justice went on, quite improperly, to introduce an entirely new assertion, namely that two days before Overbury's death Elwes had ordered his servant to bring the prisoner's best suit of hangings to his new cell, 'which you knew were your fees'. In other words, Coke was suggesting that the accused, presumably with foreknowledge of Overbury's fate, had made ready to exercise the Lieutenant's privilege of confiscating the dead man's clothing, in those days a valuable perquisite.

It was a telling point and Coke followed it by his masterstroke. He 'produced out of his bosom' like a conjuror with a rabbit a confession which, he said, Franklin had volunteered to him at five o'clock that very morning, 'as one afflicted in conscience'. Despite the fact that the document contained little to incriminate Elwes in the murder, the jury seem to have been impressed by its dramatic last minute appearance; even more so by the fact that the accused, 'knew not what to answer, or to make of his own letters'. As Elwes was to write from his death cell, 'when my own pen came against me, I was not able to speak, but stood as one amazed, or that had no tongue'. His reaction was hardly surprising since this seems to have been the first time that he had been told of the confession. Ignorant of all this, the jury retired, only to return to court with a verdict of guilty.

While awaiting execution, the former Lieutenant of the Tower opened his heart for the first time. He is said to have admitted to the priests sent to comfort him that 'he knew and concealed the wretched purpose to poison Sir Thomas Overbury', keeping it secret out of a desire for worldly advancement. When Weston warned him that he would have to poison his prisoner, he had replied, 'Let it be done so I know not of it'. He had examined his life, he said, and 'found myself to be a most horrible, filthy, vile, and beastly sinner, and one that had abused all the gifts and graces that ever God of his mercy had bestowed on me'. He went on to confess that '[m]any things had slipped his pen suspiciously and unadvisedly, whereof he can make no good account and that in some of them there was matter sufficient to condemn him'.[6] It seemed almost as if he was regretting, not his part in a murder plot, but his carelessness in having made incriminating admissions.

At six o'clock in the morning, four days after he had been sentenced to death, Elwes walked to the gallows at Tower Hill between two ministers. It was a concession to the condemned

---

[6] Andrew Amos, *The Great Oyer of Poisoning: The Trial of the Earl of Somerset for the possible poisoning of Sir Thomas Overbury* (London, Richard Bentley, 1846).

man; Tyburn was for humbler folk than a former Lieutenant of the Tower and a gibbet had to be built specially for the occasion. He went to his death with a befitting sense of style, 'arrayed in a black suit and black jerkin, with hanging sleeves, having on his head a crimson sattin cap, laced from the top downwards and roundabout, under that a black hat with a broad ribbon and ruff band, thick couched with a lace and a pair of three soled shoes'.

Standing on the scaffold, Elwes complained that the ladder was too steep for him to make the customary address of the condemned; its angle was adjusted accordingly. After making a full confession to the assembled throng he offered his thanks to the King and his Council for mercifully remitting his forfeited estate to his relatives. He had, he said, 'by divers tricks [been] drawn into this action, which I received from the Earl of Northampton and Sir Thomas Monson, and none other' (an apparent retreat from his accusation against Suffolk). He was, he said, 'flesh as any others ... and faint hearted to look death in the face'. When he spoke of leaving his friends, some of whom were present in the crowd, 'tears stood in his eyes'. After making the conventional expression of regret for his sins and exhortation to others to repent theirs, Elwes asked the hangman, who was perched on the gibbet above his head, if he might answer questions from the crowd. When this curious request was refused the condemned man gave the customary reward to the boy who held his cloak, and the noose was placed around his neck. He uttered the pre-arranged watchword, 'Lord Jesus receive my soul' and threw himself off the ladder. The executioner and his assistant each pulled on one of his legs and his end was swift.

Elwes' question to the court as to whether 'concealing without malice' was murder deserved better consideration than it received, but even if it had been accepted as a correct statement of the law, the jury might have taken the view that, as he was to admit, he had been in the plot up to his neck: we will never know. It is always possible that Elwes' admissions in the face of eternity had more to do with the mercy which the King had extended to his relatives than to any regard for the truth. But none of this alters the fact that the prosecution's case had been thin as paper; even the spectators had expected a not guilty verdict. That it was not forthcoming speaks volumes about seventeenth-century notions of justice. The former Lieutenant seems to have been convicted, as he sought to argue before the court, of no more than turning a blind eye.

But even accepting his story at its face value, Elwes' behaviour was inexcusable. He was from the outset aware of an intention to apply improper pressure to a prisoner in his care and later discovered a plot to kill the man. He actively supported the former and did nothing about the latter, save reprimand the putative poisoner and frustrate his subsequent endeavours.

Although many at the time expressed sympathy for Elwes, Carr probably got it right when he described him in a letter to the King as 'the worst deserver in this business; an unoffended instrument might have prevented all after-mischief, who for his own ends suffered it, and by the like arts afterward betrayed it'.

FRANKLIN'S TRIAL: 'I'LL NEVER NAME THEM WHILE I BREATHE'

By comparison with that of the other accused, Franklin's trial at the Court of King's Bench was almost indecently brief. Guilty he undoubtedly was, but the conduct of the proceedings raises serious questions concerning the integrity of the prosecution.

The case against Franklin consisted entirely of written and oral confessions to the investigators – the report in *The State Trials* is not always clear as to which are which – and this presents a problem. According to that report, the account given to the court comprised 'all the materials in Franklin's confession', yet the summary which appears in the report differs in numerous and significant respects from that which Coke had given at Elwes' trial a mere eleven days earlier, notably as to the nature of the poison to be used.

At his own trial, the court was told of Franklin's claim that Mrs Turner asked him first to obtain a poison which 'should not kill a man presently but lie in his body for a certain time, wherewith he might languish away little by little'. He had brought her aqua fortis to be tried on a cat. '[I]t pitifully cried for the space of two days and then died'. Apparently dissatisfied with this as 'too violent a water', Mrs Turner asked, 'What think you of white arsenick?'. Franklin replied that it was 'too violent'. Her next suggestion was powder of diamonds, but when he professed ignorance of its effects she called him a fool. This is an entirely different story from that given at the earlier trial of Elwes, when Franklin was quoted as saying that, 'Mrs Turner came to me from the Countess and wished me from her to get *the strongest poison I could* for Sir Thomas Overbury. Accordingly, I bought seven ...' (emphasis added). Either Frances asked Franklin to get a slow acting or a quick acting poison; she could hardly have asked for both.[7]

When asked by the court what he had to say in answer to the charges, Franklin confessed to having bought the poisons, but 'protested his ignorance what they meant to do with them'. It was simply not credible and it took only a quarter of an hour for the jury to bring in a guilty verdict. After passing sentence of death, Coke added another of his cryptic remarks, 'That knowing as much as he knew, if this had not been found out, neither the court, city, nor any particular family had escaped the malice of this wicked cruelty'.

It seems to have been all of a part with the judge's paranoid fears of Rome. If this suspicion had any basis outside Coke's fevered imagination, it could only have come from rumours that

---

[7] We should remember that 'Cunning' Mary had accused Frances of asking her to get her a slow acting poison.

Passion, Poison and Power

he had heard out of court: certainly, there is no foundation for the claim in the evidence that was produced at any of the Overbury trials.

But Franklin was not to die immediately. Anxious no doubt to prolong his earthly span, the condemned man continued to feed stories of an increasingly bizarre nature to the chaplains who had been sent (ostensibly) to give him spiritual comfort while awaiting death. He claimed, for example, that:

> 'there were greater persons in this matter than were yet known, and so in truth then, said he, "there are;" and that, "although the Chief Justice has found and sifted out as much as any man could, yet that he is much awry, and has not come to the ground of the business, for more were to be poisoned and murdered than are yet known, and he marvelleth that they have not been poisoned and murdered all this while.'[8]

Franklin even went so far as to hint that the King had had his son, the Prince, murdered by 'an outlandish physician and an outlandish apothecary'. Despite the improbability of these stories they seem to have made an impression on the one man who held his fate in his hands. Amos recorded how 'Sir Edward Coke, to whom these fairytales were reported, began to see red and dream o' nights of poison in every dish'. He wrote to the King, explaining that the condemned man's life had been 'reserved for a time to give light to this work of darkness ... after a convenient time when as much as can be extracted from him as can be, execution shall be done and Your Majesty never troubled therewith'.

Coke gave some hint of the nature of his suspicions when he reported to the King his fears of 'some wicked attempt (beside this villainy) against some that be dear and near unto you, and besides

---

[8] Andrew Amos, *The Great Oyer of Poisoning: The Trial of the Earl of Somerset for the possible poisoning of Sir Thomas Overbury* (London, Richard Bentley, 1846), p. 227.

some probable suspicions are given of some other persons, I will not say of what sex they be, to have had an hand in this crying sin of poisoning'. It has been suggested that this may have referred to a newsletter of 21 November 1615 which reported an unnamed bishop giving thanks for the discovery of a plot involving Franklin and Mrs Turner to poison the King, Queen, Prince and Council 'at the christening of the Lady of Somerset's child at a banquet'.[9] No evidence of such a plot has ever emerged.

Franklin's stratagem finally lost all credibility even with the gullible Coke and he followed Elwes to the gallows. Even at the brink of eternity, however, he did his best to play the fool with the hangman and had to be quietened down. His final shot, was to pat his waiting coffin and claim that, 'There are yet some left behind and great ones too, but let that pass. I'll never name them while I breathe'. That at least proved to be true.

THE ONE WHO GOT AWAY

The last of the 'small fry' to be tried turned out to be the most difficult to convict, for reasons which are obscure to this day. Sir Thomas Monson, by then Master of the Armoury in the Tower of London, was a Catholic recusant, which in the eyes of many was enough to make him suspect of any wickedness. His trial at the Guildhall was every bit as speedy as Franklin's, but with an entirely different outcome.

The first attempt to arraign (that is to say, formally charge) the accused at the Guildhall was stopped before it began, ostensibly on the ground of disorder among the crowd who had come to

---

[9] Alastair James Bellany, *The Politics of Court Scandal in Early Modern England: News Culture and the Overbury Affair, 1603–1660* (Cambridge, Cambridge University Press, 2002).

witness the event. But this may have been no more than an official prevarication: the prosecution still lacked sufficient evidence to begin the trial. The day before (29 November) Coke had written to the King with a different story. The delay in bringing Monson to trial, he wrote, was not because 'of any innocence I find in him, but that I am really persuaded he can discover secrets worthy and necessary to be known, and he may be a good witness in some points which he affirmeth against the Countess, and upon her examination had deemed, which may be a mean to whet her tongue against him'. In other words, as well as being a useful witness against Frances, Coke clung to his belief that there were great and sinister secrets which the prisoner could be persuaded to reveal.

When Monson was eventually brought to trial on 4 December, he pleaded not guilty to a charge of conspiring with Franklin to murder Overbury. But before the prosecution could even open their case the accused interrupted the proceedings to ask the court's permission to call Frances' father, Thomas Howard, to court to answer two questions. He wanted him, first, to confirm that it was Northampton and not himself who had chosen Elwes as Lieutenant of the Tower, and, secondly, to confirm that Elwes had been selected for this post 'as an instrument to make Overbury submissive to My Lord Treasurer and his house for the former wrongs done to them'. (Monson also asked that Sir Robert Cotton should be present in court, but in the hurly burly which followed his intervention this request seems to have been overlooked.)

In yet another of his curious outbursts Chief Justice Coke chose this moment to criticize the conduct, even the motives, of the prosecution. After the customary genuflection to the King's most excellent majesty and grace he expressed his surprise at the half-hearted investigation of the case. It had, he said, been:

> 'so mild a proceeding in so great an affair: for neither the great man's house in the Tower, nor his lady's house nor this prisoner's house (to my knowledge) have been searched, neither hath this

prisoner been committed to the sheriff, but to an alderman, a man who of all others might be most kind to him; for, as I take it lest I should be mistaken, sir Francis Anderson married sir Stephen Some's daughter, and sir Thomas Monson married sir Francis Anderson's sister; I never knew the like favour, nor do I like it so well, but do declare it as a gentle proceeding from the King. For other things, I dare not discover secrets; but though there was no house searched, yet such letters were produced, which make our deliverance as great as any that happened to the children of Israel.'

It was a curious observation from the bench at the outset of a criminal trial, not least because of the suggestion that the King was deliberately going easy on the accused.

In any event Monson ignored Coke's odd intervention and renewed his request to have the Lord Treasurer called as a witness. Coke's response was to read aloud a letter which Howard had sent him (obviously with fore-knowledge of the prisoner's request), 'I have heard that sir Thomas Monson thinks I can clear him, but I know nothing of him to accuse or excuse him; but I hope he is not guilty of so foul a crime'. 'You hear', said Coke addressing the accused, 'that he will neither accuse you, nor excuse you'. But, in truth, Howard's letter was an equivocating response which failed to address the questions which the prisoner had posed. He persisted, 'I do not accuse the Lord Treasurer, nor calumniate him, for I know he is very honourable, but I desire to have an answer to my two questions'. Coke merely responded, 'You shall hear more of that when the time serveth', and asked the accused to acknowledge his sin. Monson replied with passion, 'If I be guilty I renounce the King's mercy and God's. I am innocent'. Coke could only mutter peevishly that, 'there was more against you than you know of'.

When Monson continued to insist on his innocence Coke responded by calling him 'popish'. Mr Prosecutor Hyde could not refrain from adding his pennyworth, 'I have looked into this business and I protest, my lord, he is as guilty as the guiltiest'. Here, the trial seems to tail off, never to be resumed. Coke's petty revenge was to order that the prisoner be led back to the Tower in the pouring rain.[10]

Afterwards, Coke wrote to the King justifying the discontinuance of the proceedings. '[C]ontrary to the expectation who thought he would have stand mute', he wrote, Monson had 'put himself upon God and the country and *seeing we meant not to procede* we take that course that your justice might in no sort be blemished ... it was signified that by the goodness of God very lately some such further discovery had been made (which was as yet a secret) we thought not fit to procede with him at this time' (emphasis added). It was a cryptic remark arising more likely from deliberate obfuscation than seventeenth-century literary style.

But Coke's dark suspicions did not stop with the papists. During the trial, he had remarked, 'God knows what became of that sweet babe, Prince Harry, but I know somewhat'. This was Weldon's version: according to *The State Trials* he went much further, 'The Lord Chief Justice having at this trial let drop some insinuations that Overbury's death had somewhat in it of retaliation, as if he had been guilty of the same crime against prince Henry'.[11] It was almost as if he was suggesting that James had had a hand in the murder. As the report goes on to note, Coke 'was rebuked for his indiscretion and before the next year expired removed from his post'.

In October 1616, long after fears of a popish plot had subsided, Bacon recommended that Monson be pardoned on the ground that the evidence against him was 'doubtful' and 'conjectural'. Even Coke was prevailed upon to acknowledge the man's innocence, though whether out of conviction or political necessity is hard to know. After Monson had been pardoned and released from the

---

[10] Some dispute this story, but it is consistent with Coke's attitude towards the prisoner.
[11] Sir Simonds D'Ewes reports that this allegation was prevalent among the Scots.

'A Net to Catch Little Fishes'

Tower he declared himself 'guiltless of the blood of that man for which I stand here indicted, guiltless of the fact, guiltless of the procurement thereof, guiltless of the privity or consent thereto, directly or indirectly'. Four years later he was re-admitted to the royal presence, exonerated but hardly untainted.

It is still a mystery why Monson's trial was brought to so inconclusive an end. It was James himself who seems to have taken the decision, ostensibly for lack of evidence. Weldon tells the story of how:

> 'The night before he was to come to his tryall, the King, being at the game of Maw,[12] said, To-morrow comes Tom Monson to his tryall; Yea, said the King's Card-holder, where if he doe not play his master-prize your Majesty shall never trust me; this so run in the King's minde, as the next game he said he was sleepy, and would play out that set next night; the Gentleman departed to his lodging, but was no sooner gone, but the King sent for him; what communication they had I knew not, (yet it may be can more easily guess than any other), but it is most certaine, next under God, that Gentleman saved his life, for the King sent a post presently to London, to let the Lord Chiefe Justice know he would see Monson's examination and confession, to see if it were worthy to touch his life for so small a matter; Monson was too wise to set anything but faire in his confession; what he would have stab'd with should have been (viva voce) at his arraignment. The King sent word he saw nothing worthy of death, or of bonds, in his accusation or examination.'

The reference to the possibility of Monson making some sort of revelation (or 'stabbing') at his trial hints tantalizingly that he too, like Carr, may have been the possessor of knowledge which James did not wish to be made public. It is an intriguing idea which the historian, Samuel Gardiner has undermined by noting that when the royal conversation took place James was at Newmarket and that there was no time for all this to come out in the space of a

---

[12] Maw was James' favourite card game.

Passion, Poison and Power

single night.[13] How then should we view Monson's involvement in the Overbury tragedy?

Coke claimed that Monson knew as much of the plot as any man living, and little wonder. He was a known supporter of Northampton, and he had recommended the appointment of Weston as Overbury's gaoler. Some of the contaminated food had been brought to Overbury into the Tower by one of his former employees. He had restricted the flow of letters in and out of the prisoner's cell. And (though the connection is less immediate) his daughter was the most popular candidate for Frances' veiled substitute at the virginity test.[14] Elwes appears at first sight to have taken two different views of Monson's guilt. In his 'apology' he declared 'in this business, in my conscience, [Monson] is as clear as my own soul', whereas on the gallows he claimed that he had been drawn into 'this action' by 'the earl of Northampton and Sir Thomas Monson'. There may be no inconsistency in these statements if the 'business' which he referred to in his apology was merely the tricking of Overbury into the Tower, whereas the 'action' he referred to at his execution was the prisoner's murder by poisoning. He may have been telling the truth on both counts.

Now only the two leading players remained on the stage.

---

[13] Samuel R. Gardiner, *History of England from the Accession of James I to the Outbreak of the Civil War, 1603–1642,* Vol. 2 (London, Longman, Green and Co, 1883).
[14] It probably has no bearing on Overbury's fate, but it is a curious fact that Monson's brother William had for many years been a patient of Dr Forman.

ACT 8

THE FALL OF THE HOUSE OF SOMERSET

When in October 1615, the Commissioners heard of Carr's 'great contempt' in issuing the illegal warrant they immediately took steps to ensure that the couple would remain available for questioning. The Earl was instructed to keep strictly to his chambers 'near the cockpit at Whitehall' and not to receive visitors. Frances was told to stay at her home in Blackfriars or at Lord Knollys' house near the tiltyard. (The Commissioner's letter began, somewhat incongruously, by offering their 'very hearty commendations to your Lordship', and was signed, 'Your very loving friends'.) At the same time they declared to the King their intention 'with all convenient speed to enter into an examination of the Earl and Countess'.

Shortly afterwards, the Commissioners wrote to the King notifying him that their investigations had given rise to 'vehement suspicion' and 'matter ... pregnant' against the Earl of being accessory before the fact to the murder. It was enough for James to have the Earl stripped of his seals of office and thrown into the Tower. Frances was saved from this plight only by virtue of the fact that she was pregnant.

Carr's interrogation began at the end of October. Apparently (for we have no record of the interviews), he admitted that he had sent powder to Overbury in the Tower, but asserted that it was a 'wholesome and good physic'. And he confirmed that he

Passion, Poison and Power

had urged Elwes' appointment as Lieutenant at Northampton's behest. Critical to the case against the Earl were the letters he had received from the King, Northampton and Overbury, and given to Sir Robert Cotton for safe keeping. They had been put into a locked cabinet and handed over to a friend. By various vicissitudes the cabinet had come into the hands of Coke who ordered that it be broken open. The letters written by the King were returned to their author and were never seen again. On discovering that some of the remaining correspondence had been tampered with, Cotton was taken into custody for questioning, only to be released without charge six months after the trials were over.

Frances, now heavy with child, was the next to be questioned. At this stage she still retained enough of her fiery spirit to express resentment at the way in which Coke had allowed details of her pre-marital affair with Carr to be made public. She freely admitted sending tarts and jellies to Overbury during his imprisonment, but strenuously denied any involvement in his death. Further questioning was suspended to allow her to give birth and on 9 December 1615 she was delivered of a daughter, which she diplomatically named Anne after the Queen. A few months later Frances, still at liberty, was unwise enough to appear at court. It was a provocation too far on the part of someone under investigation for murder and on 4 April 1616 she, too, was committed to the Tower and her child put in the care of her parents. Chilled at the prospect of entering the ancient prison, Frances begged that she should not be put in the chamber where Overbury had died; instead, she was accommodated, first in the quarters of the new Lieutenant of the Tower, Sir George More, and later in the room recently vacated by Sir Walter Raleigh on his departure for the ill-fated Orinoco expedition.[1]

All the while this was going on James had been trying to persuade Carr to admit his guilt, but was getting nowhere.[2] When in December 1615 the Earl asked to see the King about a 'great matter' James joyfully assumed that he had changed his mind and despatched Lord Knollys and James Hay, Carr's former patron, to the Tower to find out exactly what he had in mind. It proved to be no more than his usual complaint that he and his wife deserved more comfortable lodgings on the ground that he was not accused of the grave crime of treason, but 'only' of murder. A week later James wrote to Carr and instructed his new Lieutenant of the Tower to read the letter out to him. Carr had not been ill-used, James wrote; on the contrary, his remaining at large had caused 'a great murmur among the people that justice was stayed'. His crime was not simply murder, but 'murther of the fowlest kind' and 'the suspico[n] against hym so vehement, and the proofes so pregnant'.[3] (James was well aware that the last statement was untrue, otherwise the Earl would already have been standing in the dock.) Finally, the letter reminded Carr how the common people had rejoiced at the execution of Weston, a fate which, the King

---

[1] Raleigh had been lodged in the thirteenth-century Bloody Tower under sentence of death for treason, but was released in order to go to South America to search for the treasures of the legendary city of El Dorado. His expedition was unsuccessful, a failure which was made worse by his destroying a Spanish town on the Orinoco river in disobedience to the King's instructions. Arriving back in England, he was immediately returned to the Tower to be beheaded on the earlier charge.

[2] Much later, James was to tell a correspondent that Carr had 'confessed to the chief justice [at about this time] that his cause was so evil likely as he knew no jury could acquit him' (Letter to Sir George More, 13 May 1616). Unfortunately, we have no independent confirmation of this intriguing 'confession'.

[3] Letter of 29 December 1615 printed in *Archeologia*, Society of Antiquaries of London.

Passion, Poison and Power

implied, could soon be his if he did not show contrition and admit his guilt.

Carr showed no signs of cracking, so James turned his attention to what he believed to be the weaker vessel. He wrote to Frances, offering her mercy if only she would only plead guilty and show herself penitent. It worked; shortly after Christmas 1615 the Countess asked the King to send two people to whom she could unburden herself. Viscount Fenton and the Earl of Montgomery duly attended to receive her confession. Unfortunately, this document has not survived (if, indeed, the confession was ever reduced to writing). Our only clue to its contents is the Spanish ambassador's report to his King to the effect that Frances admitted desiring and aiding in Overbury's death, 'as being a girl aggrieved and offended by the most unworthy things which [Overbury] had said about her person'. The same source reports her denying that her husband was aware of the plot, a denial which she was to maintain strenuously to the end. Robert, when he learned of her confession, could only say that 'he was sorry [she] was guilty of so foul a fact'.

Nevertheless, with Frances' confession in his hands, the King felt confident enough to act and on 19 January 1616 the couple were formally indicted by a grand jury as 'accessories to murder before the fact done' and committed to stand their trial.[4] It came as a great shock to the Earl, and on 7 February in an attempt to salvage what he could from the shipwreck of his life, he wrote a desperate letter to the King: 'Being told by my Lord Chief Justice that I was indicted, and was shortly to expect my arraignment, I did not then believe him, for I did not look for that way'. He begged not to be put on trial on the ground that he had committed

---

[4] An accessory before the fact was someone who counselled or procured a crime but was not present at its actual commission.

The Fall of the House of Somerset

no offence against his monarch or the state. 'But if I must come to my trial', he went on:

> 'knowing the presumptions may be strong against me in respect I consented to and endeavoured the imprisonment of Sir T. Overbury (though I designed it for his reformation, not his ruin) I therefore desire your Majesty's mercy, and that you will be pleased to give me leave to dispose of my lands and goods to my wife and child, and graciously to pardon her, having confessed the fact.'

It was too late; the plea was not even answered; instead, James sent Commissioners to tell the prisoner that, though his own trial could not be far off, it was not too late to seek mercy. They were instructed to make no promise, but, in the Commissioners' words, 'did assure him, that your majesty was compassionate of him if he gave you some ground whereon to work; that as long as he stood upon his innocency and trial, your majesty was tied in honour to proceed according to justice ...'. Carr would have none of the offer and continued to protest his innocence. However, he begged the King once again to refrain from prosecuting Frances as the mother of his child, a request that he must have known could not possibly be acceded to.

It only remained to decide who should prosecute the noble couple.

COKE REPLACED AS PROSECUTOR

Coke may have been a great lawyer, but he was a blunt and tactless human being. Some years before he had offended the scholarly James deeply by declaring that 'God had endowed His Majesty with excellent science, and great endowments of nature; but his Majesty was not learned in the laws of his realm of England ... which law is an act which requires long study and experience, be-

Passion, Poison and Power

fore that a man can attain to the cognizance of it'.[1] His failure to keep the King abreast of his inquiries in the Overbury case had not endeared him to James, and, as we have seen, he had a bee in his bonnet.

At the time, England was in one of its periodic lathers about Roman Catholicism. (Not entirely without reason. The Saint Bartholomew's day massacre of Protestants and Catholic Spain's attempted invasion of England had not disappeared from folk memory.[2]) Fears of revanchist Romanism and re-invigorated Spanish nationalism were rife. All sorts of rumours were going around, including one of a 'ship of pocket pistols [coming] out of Spain and that it was intended by the Papists to have made a massacre'.[3] Coke shared the popular fear and had given voice to it publicly at the trials of Franklin and Monson. He had accused Anne Turner of being a Papist, and in Elwes' trial had raised the bogey of the Spanish armada. Overbury's death, he believed, was part of another Romish plot against the English King and his peoples.

Carr was by descent and inclination sympathetic to Roman Catholicism. He was a known supporter of rapprochement rather than confrontation with Spain, and in 1614 he had entered into negotiations with the Spanish ambassador with a view to finding a dynastic marriage for the young Prince Charles, who, on his brother Henry's death, had become the heir apparent. Although James was aware of what was afoot it seems that Carr, aided by his friend Cotton, had made offers to Spain which had not been authorized by the King. To Coke, the Earl's actions smelt like treasonable dealings with a foreign power. In fact there was nothing sinister

---

[1] In the case known as *Prohibitions del Roy,* 1607. A *prohibition del roy* was one that denied the king's jurisdiction.
[2] On 23 August 1572 the Paris mob had murdered some thousands of Protestants, known as Huguenots, in an organized massacre.
[3] Michael Sparke.

The Fall of the House of Somerset

in them; even James could see that his investigator was chasing rainbows.

So far as the King was concerned, the last straw was the Chief Justice's outrageous hint from the Bench that Overbury had been killed in retaliation for his having murdered the Prince. It was enough for him to be stripped of his responsibilities in the case. (The official reason given was Coke's intransigence in matters affecting the royal privilege.) In his stead, the King appointed the Attorney General, Francis Bacon, to prosecute the unhappy couple. Whatever his faults – and they were manifold – Bacon had an intellect every bit as subtle as Coke's and he set about his task with a will. To make the charges stick, he meticulously reviewed all his predecessor's interviews and re-examined witness after witness with a care that befitted the author of the *Essays*. The fruits of his work are contained in the extraordinarily detailed plan for the strategic conduct of the trials which he sent to the King on 28 April 1614. Fortunately, this document has survived, endorsed with James' perceptive responses to each of its proposals. The first question to be decided, wrote Bacon, was what to do if Carr made a full confession. He ran through the options. To call off the trials, he suggested, would 'save them both from the stage and that public ignominy'; to proceed with the trials but stay or reprieve the judgment would 'save the lands from forfeiture and the blood from corruption'; and to proceed to conviction would 'save the blood only, not from corrupting, but from spilling'. James declared that he would choose between the first and the last options when he knew whether Carr was willing to confess or not.

Having dropped Coke's foolish notion of charging the Earl with treason Bacon realized that, if he were to prepare the ground for his eventual pardon, it was necessary 'so to moderate the manner of charging him, as it might make him not odious beyond the extent of mercy'. James saw the wisdom in this, observing, 'Ye will do well to remember likewise in your preamble that only zeal to justice maketh me take this course. I have commandit you not to expatiate, nor digresse upon any other points, that maye not serve clearly for probation or inducement of that point, whereof he is accused'. Plans were even laid for how the court should respond if, like Weston, the prisoner refused to take part in the proceedings. In the end, Bacon opined sagely that the most likely outcome to the proceedings was that 'the lady confess and that Somerset himself plead not guilty and be found guilty'. James responded by instructing that if Carr should be acquitted of murder he should be remanded to the Tower as close prisoner to be questioned about 'many high and heinous offences, *though not capital*' (emphasis added). It would be fascinating to know what he had in mind.

Bacon next had to decide how the prosecution case should be presented in court. The result was a forensic *tour de force*. The lawyer, Amos, admiringly observed that the proofs were 'distributed under four heads, the first head having four subordinate divisions, and the second being presented under "eight points of a compass", each matter, according to the degree of its intricacy or its importance, being exhibited in a 'single, double or reflex light'. The Earl was to be allowed three opportunities for 'cogitation' upon each piece of evidence as it was brought forward, namely 'to take aim, to ruminate, and readvise'. It was, Amos concluded, 'perhaps the most remarkable specimen, in ancient or modern trials, of the Genius of Order presiding over a systematic arrangement of evidence'. It was a task for which Bacon was eminently qualified. (As he was to tell the peers, 'I love order'.)

Determined not to repeat Coke's clumsy treatment of his master, Bacon reported his progress almost daily, either to the King or to Villiers. James' responses were always considered and helpful. Reading them today, it is apparent that he genuinely believed in Carr's guilt and was determined to see him convicted, though equally determined to spare him the ultimate penalty if that were consistent with his view of justice (a view, we should remember,

The Fall of the House of Somerset

in which nobles were somehow entitled to gentler treatment than mere commoners).

Bacon's next problem was how he the court should react if Frances entered the expected plea of guilty. In particular, he was determined that nothing should be said that would cause her to 'break forth into passionate protestations for [her husband's] clearing'. In a letter to Villiers of 10 May 1616 he wrote, 'my Lord Chancellor and I have devised that upon the entrance into that declaration [that is, of guilt] she shall, in respect of her weakness, and not to add farther affliction, be withdrawn'. Her womanly frailty in other words was to be used as an excuse for bustling Frances out of court should she attempt to blurt out anything that might serve to exonerate her husband.

The final step in Bacon's preparations was to seek the views of the judges of the King's Bench on the strength of the evidence and how it should be presented. Alien though such a course may seem inappropriate to modern eyes, it was then common practice in cases of importance. After three or four hours' discussion the judges agreed that 'drawing [Carr] onto trial is most honourable and just, and that the evidence is good and fair'. If, as expected, Frances were to plead guilty and keep quiet, they advised, 'no evidence ought to be given' at her trial.

Meanwhile, the repeated adjournments of the Somersets' trials had caused widespread concern and speculation. Was the reason for the delay, people asked, fear of a Spanish conspiracy as Coke had hinted, or was it because the trials might somehow embarrass the King? In fact neither of these suspicions was well founded; everything was being done to bring the cases to trial, but there were real problems in the way. Frances' trial had been delayed by her pregnancy and Carr's because of his adamant refusal to make the confession without which, Bacon was only too well aware, the case against him was weak.

At his wit's end, James turned to his trusted friend, Sir George More, and on 9 May wrote asking him to see the prisoner in secret 'in a thing greatly concerning my honour and service'. The King desired to make Carr confess to murder, he wrote, in order to 'leave some place for my mercy to work upon'. The importance and delicacy of this task are evident from the fact that these instructions were written in James' own hand. More did what he could, but without success. A few days later the King wrote again to his Lieutenant, regretting that his prisoner:

> 'turns all the great care I have of him not only against himself, but against me also, as far as he can ... Give him assurance in my name, that if he will yet, before his trial, confess cheerily unto the Commissioners his guiltiness of this fact, I will not only perform what I promised by my last messenger both towards him and his wife, but I will enlarge it, according to the phrase of the civil law, &c. ... Assure him, that I protest upon my honour my end in this is for his and his wife's good.'

This virtuous sentiment was spoiled somewhat by the King's next suggestion, that More should tell Carr, as if of his own volition, that he feared Carr's wife should 'plead weakly for his innocency', but that 'the Commissioners have, ye know not how, some secret assurance that in the end she will confess of him—but this must only be as from yourself'. The letter, which was dated 16 May, ended, 'Let none living know of this'. It was a deceitful and dishonorable stratagem on James' part which could only have been born out of desperation. To the King's frustration, Carr remained adamant and nothing came of the offer.

Negotiations continued with a view to persuading, even bullying, the prisoner into admitting his guilt. Although the King could make no promises, the Earl was told, a confession would make His Majesty more likely to be merciful; otherwise the consequences would be dire. When Bacon assured him of the King's determination to secure him in life and fortune, Carr replied, 'Life and fortune are not worth the acceptance, when honour is gone', adding that he was 'neither Gowrie nor Balmerino', a biting reference to two men whom James was believed to have treated badly.[4] Reporting the Earl's reaction, Bacon wrote, '(W)hen we asked him some question that did touch the prince or some foreign practice, which we did very sparingly at this time, yet he grew a little stirred, but in the questions of the empoisonment very cold and modest'. (Apparently, 'cold and modest' was how Bacon interpreted the attitude of someone determinedly protesting his innocence.) Throughout his dealings with the prisoner Bacon took great care that nothing the King said or wrote could be traceable back to the throne. In a letter to Villiers he wrote, '... the glimmering of that which the King hath done to others, by way of talk to him, cannot hurt as I conceive; but I would not have that part of the message as from the King, but added by the messenger as from himself'.

Realizing at last that there was no hope of Carr budging on the issue of his guilt and with Frances' confession now in the bag, Bacon decided that there was no reason to delay further. And so it was that Frances was the first of the Somersets to be brought to judgment.

---

[4] The Earl of Gowrie and his son were killed after apparently having tried to kill or kidnap King James. The full truth of this strange event has never come to light. Lord Balmerino was a Scottish judge who falsely confessed to having forged a letter from James to the Pope when revelation of its true authorship would have been embarrassing to the King.

ACT 9

THE SOMERSETS ON TRIAL

On 24 May 1616, the twenty-six-year-old Frances Countess of Somerset was rowed along the Thames from the Tower to the Palace of Westminster to be arraigned as accessory before the fact to the murder of Sir Thomas Overbury. In the boat with her was a gentleman porter with his axe, the blade turned away from her as befitted an unconvicted prisoner. Upon arrival, Frances and her escort were ushered into the Great Hall of the Palace. It was crowded with onlookers anxious to hear revelations of scandal; seats could not be had, even at silly prices. Discreetly hidden among the banks of spectators was Frances' former husband, Robert.

As a noblewoman, Frances was entitled to be tried by her peers in the court of the Lord High Steward. On this occasion the Lord Chancellor, Lord Ellesmere, had been assigned that role. On the bench beside him sat twenty-two Peers of the Realm, carefully chosen by Bacon in consultation with the King. They included the Lord Privy Seal, Edward Somerset Earl of Worcester and the new Lord Chamberlain, William Herbert, Earl of Pembroke. Legal input was provided by Lord Chief Justice Coke and seven judges at law. The proceedings had all the trappings of theatre. When the Lord Chancellor entered the court:

'... there came before him six Serjeants at arms, with their maces; sir Geo. Coppin with his patent; sir Rd. Coningsby with his white staff; Mr Manwaring with the great seal; he himself, at the upper end of the court, sitting; under a cloth of estate; on both hands of him the peers, under them the judges; at the farther end the King's counsel, below the judges; on one side Finch, keeper of the records of attainders; the clerk of the crown and his deputy, in the midst of the court, the serjeant-crier standing by him; sir Rd. Coningsby, sir Geo. Coppin, the seal-bearer, &c. at my Lord Steward's feet. The Prisoner at the Bar behind the King's counsel; the Lieutenant of the Tower in a little place adjoining to the Bar.'

The trial began with the court's patent being presented on bended knee to the Lord High Steward amid repeated shouts of 'Oyez'.[1] The prisoner was then led to the bar where she 'made three reverences to his grace and the peers'. She was dressed 'in black stammel [the garb of penitents], a cypress chaperon [or hood], a cobweb lawn ruff and cuffs'. As someone accustomed to being able to satisfy her every whim, Frances found herself in an unfamiliar state of dependency. Her great uncle, the powerful Northampton, was dead, her husband was in prison awaiting trial, and her parents had retired in shame to Audley End; her very existence was in the hands of strangers. As the indictment was read out she 'stood, looking pale, trembled, and shed some few tears; and at the first naming of Weston in the indictment, put her fan before her face, and there held it half covered till the indictment was read'.

The clerk of the crown demanded, 'Frances, Countess of Somerset, what sayest thou? Art thou guilty of this felony and murder, or not guilty?'. Frances bobbed a curtsy to the Lord High Steward, and answered 'Guilty' with a low voice, 'but wonderful fearful'. Asked what she had to say in mitigation, she replied in words so soft that they had to be repeated to the court, 'I can much aggravate, but nothing extenuate my fault; I desire mercy, and

---

[1] Pronounced 'O-yes'. Norman French for 'Hear ye'.

that the lords will intercede for me to the King'. The modestly crafted language was exactly what the prosecution had hoped to hear, almost as if it had been prepared and carefully rehearsed at their prompting. Attorney General Bacon announced his joy at the accused's noble gesture in so frankly acknowledging her guilt, and compared it favourably to her accomplices who had wasted the court's time by protesting their innocence.

Bacon's original intention had been to outline the facts of the case to the court, as was customary after a plea of guilty. In a letter to Villiers he had written:

> '[If] the Lady will confess the indictment; ..., no evidence ought to be given. But because it shall not be a dumb shew, and for his Majesty's honour in so solemn an Assembly, I purpose to make a declaration of the proceedings of this great work of justice, from the beginning to the end, wherein, nevertheless, I will be careful no ways to prevent or discover the evidence of the next day.'

But nothing like this took place, seemingly on the advice of the judges. Although Frances pleaded guilty as expected, not a word was uttered publicly about the manner of Overbury's death or Frances' role in it. After referring briefly to the circumstances in which the murder had come to light Bacon merely declared, 'The King still endeavours to search the truth of this business'. Conscious of this glaring omission the editors of *The State Trials* sought to remedy it by reproducing for their readers that which had been denied to the court, the lengthy address which Bacon had prepared for a not guilty plea, but for those present in court the proceedings were for all intents and purposes the 'dumb shew' which he had first determined to forswear.

The elderly Lord Chancellor was then handed his staff of office and pronounced sentence, albeit accompanied by a heavy hint of mercy:

> 'Frances Countess of Somerset, whereas thou hast been indicted, arraigned, pleaded Guilty, and that thou hast nothing to say for

thyself, it is now my part to pronounce Judgment; only thus much before, since my lords have heard with what humility and grief you have confessed the fact, I do not doubt they will signify so much to the King, and mediate for his grace towards you: but in the mean time, according to the law, the sentence must be this, That thou shalt be carried from hence to the Tower of London, and from thence to the place of execution, where you are to be hanged by the neck till you be dead; and the Lord have mercy upon your soul.'

After the usual sycophantic tributes to the King's wisdom and mercy, Bacon reinforced the court's indication that Frances' admission of guilt might not go unrewarded. Since James had come to the throne, he observed, there had been no 'blood bath' of guilty noblemen. Nevertheless, the prisoner left court with her face to the sharp side of the axe. Her trial had been completed so swiftly she barely realized that it was over. Even the public gallery were disappointed. Bacon, however, must have breathed a sigh of relief: the elaborate precautions he had put in place to guard against the possibility of embarrassing comments being made had in the end proved to be unnecessary.

CARR REFUSES TRIAL

With Frances out of the way, it only remained to dispose of the troublesome Earl, but Carr threw the whole process into confusion. Deeply offended by the way he had been treated and still vehemently denying his guilt, he caused consternation by bluntly informing the Lieutenant of the Tower that he would take no part in his own trial. Weldon tells the story in his usual vivid way:

'And now for the last act enters Somerset himself on the stage, who being told as the manner is by the Lieutenant that he must provide to go next day to his Trial, did absolutely refuse it, and said they should carry him in his bed: that the King had assured him, he should not come to any trial, neither durst the King; to bring him to trial; this was in an high strain, and in a language not well understood by [the Lieutenant of the Tower, Sir] George More, that made More quiver and shake, and however he was accounted a wise man yet was he near at his wits end; yet away goes More to Greenwich, as late as it was, being 12 at night, bounceth at the back stairs as if mad, to whom came Jo. Loveston, one of the grooms, out of his bed, enquires the reason of that distemper at so late a season; More tells him, he must speak with the King; Loveston replies, he is quiet, which, in the Scottish dialect, is fast asleep; More says, you must awake him; More was called in (the chamber left to the King and More); he tells the King those passages, and desired to be directed by the King, for he was gone beyond his own reason to hear such bold and undutiful expressions from a faulty subject against a just sovereign: the King falls into a passion of tears. "On my soul, More, I wot not what to do, thou art a wise man, help me in this great straight, and thou shalt find thou dost it for a thankful master".'

More lived up to James' expectations. At about three o'clock that morning he returned to Carr's cell to tell him that he had found James 'full of grace in his intentions towards him ...', but that in order 'to satisfy justice you must appear, although return instantly again without any further proceeding, only you shall know your enemies and their malice, though they shall have no power over you: With this trick of wit', comments Weldon, 'he allayed his fury, and got him quietly, about eight in the morning, to the hall ...'. More's reward for this service was a suit at law to the value of £1,500; it must have seemed worth every penny to the King.

James' was still concerned that a resentful Carr might say something indiscreet in open court. To guard against this he instructed More to tell the prisoner 'roundly that if in his speeches he shall tax the King, that the justice of England is, that he shall be taken away, and the evidence shall go on without him; and then all the people will cry "away with him"; and then it shall not be in the King's will to save his life, the people will be so set on fire'.[2]

---

[2] *Letters and Life of Francis Bacon* (James Spedding et al, London, 1857).

In case this threat was not enough two trusty halberdiers were ordered to stand in court on either side of the prisoner ready to shut his mouth with a cloak and whisk him off to the Tower should he utter anything untoward.

'DEATH SHOULD BE HIS BAIL'

At last, at ten o'clock in the morning on the day after Frances' conviction and some eight months after he had first been arrested, the Earl was brought before his peers in the Great Hall at Westminster. He was carefully dressed in 'a plain black satin suit, laid with two satin laces in a seam; a gown of uncut velvet lined with unshorn: all the sleeves laid with satin lace; a pair of gloves with satin tops, his George [that is, the medal of the Order of the Garter] about his neck, his hair curled, his visage pale, his beard long, his eyes sunk in his head'. The court was crowded; among the onlookers was Essex, not discreetly as he had been at Frances' trial, but 'under the prisoner's nose'. Contemplating his judges and the other great men in court, Carr must have reflected on the time only a few short years before when so many of them, including Coke the judge and Bacon the prosecutor, had showered presents on him in hope of future favours.

The proceedings began with the same frills and trumpery as Frances' trial, with repeated shouts of 'Oyez' and multiple 'reverences' to the court. Asked to raise his hand for the reading of the indictment, Carr held it up so long that Sir George More had to tell him to put it down. (The two men were observed to whisper together on a number of occasions throughout the proceedings.) Exceptionally, the prisoner was allowed pen and ink 'to help your memory'. Stripped of its technicalities and converted from the legal Latin in which it was written, Carr was charged with procuring Weston to administer poison to Overbury from which he had died. To this, he firmly pleaded, 'not guilty'.

Serjeant Montague opened the case for the prosecution by outlining the 'four several' attempts to kill Overbury. His allegations were most particular:

- there was an attempt to poison him by red arsenic (or realgar) on 9 May 1613,
- arsenic (that is, white arsenic) was used in a second attempt in June 1613,
- mercury sublimate was used on 10 July 1613, and
- again on 14 September 1613,

resulting in the death of Overbury the following day.

Later, during the course of Carr's defence Serjeant Crew gave details of the 'powders' which Carr had sent in. 'The first [which was sent in via Killigrew] was lost; the second [Carr] sent him by Rawlins; and the third (Carr himself) took at Buly [Beaulieu]'. But, Crew went on, there was a fourth powder which was 'sent by Davis, was that that made him so sick and gave him so many stools; and that was poison, and sent three weeks after that that Rawlins carried'.

When Bacon rose to address the court he began by stressing that murder was the gravest of crimes short of treason. In this case it was particularly aggravated by the facts that death was caused by poison, that it was committed on the King's prisoner, and that it was murder 'under the colour of friendship'. He then explained how he proposed to present the case, following closely the plan which had been agreed with the King, 'First I will make a narration of the fact itself. Secondly, I will break and distribute the proofs as they concern the prisoner. And, thirdly, according to the distribution, I will produce them and read them, to use them'.

Carr, he claimed, was involved in everything concerning the plan to administer poison, he was party to the poisoning itself, he delivered poison, he constantly asked how the prisoner fared, he called for the plot to be speeded up when it seemed to lag, and, finally, his conduct after the murder showed a guilty conscience or a desire to cover up his part in the enterprise.

One of the problems facing the prosecution which they could not reveal to the court was that, if the King was to accomplish later his declared wish to pardon a convicted Carr, the trial had to be conducted in such a way as not to blacken his name unduly. As Bacon explained it to Villiers, it was necessary to paint Carr as a man 'delinquent to the peers but not odious to the people'. This could only be done by shifting much of the blame to Overbury. Bacon accordingly described the dead man to the court as:

> '[someone] that always carried himself insolently, both towards the Queen and towards the late Prince: that he was a man that carried Somerset in courses separate and opposite to the privy council; that he was a man fit to be an incendiary of a state; full of bitterness and wildness of speech and project; that he was thought also lately to govern Somerset that inasmuch that in his own letters he vaunted that from him proceeded Somerset's fortune, credit and understanding.'

It was a picture quite unrecognizable from the one that Bacon had painted of Overbury at the trial of Sir John Hollis. Then he had said that, '... the greatest fault he ever heard by [Overbury], was that he made his friend his idol'. Now he stigmatized him as a man 'of an unbounded and impudent spirit ... wholly possessed of ambition and vainglory' and 'of an insolent and thrasonical[3] disposition'. When Carr had fallen for Frances, Bacon went on, Overbury:

> 'made pretence to do the true part of a friend, for that he accounted her an unworthy woman. But the truth was, Overbury, who (to speak plainly) had little that was solid for religion, or moral virtue, but was wholly possessed with ambition and vain-glory, was loth

---

[3] 'Boastful', from a character in a play by the Roman dramatist, Terence.

to have any partners in the favour of my lord of Somerset; and especially not any of the house of the Howards, against whom he had always professed hatred and opposition.'

This, said Bacon, gave two people reason to want Overbury out of the way, the lady Frances 'in respect that he crossed her love and abused her name (which are furies in women); the other of a more deep nature from my lord of Somerset himself, who was afraid of Overbury's nature ...'. But there was, the prosecutor went on, 'a third stream, [namely] Northampton's ambition, who desires to be first in favour with my lord of Somerset; and knowing Overbury's malice to himself, and to his house, thought that man must be removed and cut off, so as certainly it was resolved and decided, that Overbury must die'.

As with the other trials, most of the prosecution case consisted of statements, or extracts from statements, or even summaries of statements made to the interrogators. The first was from Overbury's former servant, Payton, who told of seeing 'a letter of his master's, whose hand he knew, to my Lord of Somerset, wherein were these words, "If I die, my blood lie upon you."'. Another servant, Davies, declared that he had 'heard his master say that he would have gone ambassador, but that my Lord of Rochester dissuaded him'. The witness went on to describe how Overbury was accustomed to opening the King's letters and copying passages for Carr's benefit. Bacon was careful to explain that this evidence was being introduced, not because the practice was wrong in itself, but in order to show that Overbury was privy to many secrets which he could have used against the accused.

Bacon then outlined the plot whereby Overbury was to be offered 'some honourable employment in foreign parts, and should underhand, by my lord of Somerset [that is, Carr], be encouraged to refuse it; and so, upon contempt, he should be laid prisoner in the Tower, and then they thought he should be close enough, and death should be his bail'. When this first part of their plan had

The Somersets on Trial

been accomplished, Bacon went on, and Elwes and Weston were placed in control of their victim, Franklin was instructed with the help of Anne Turner ('the lay mistress of the poisons', as he called her) to 'chase him with poison after poison, poison in salt-meats, poison in sweet-meats, poison in medicines and vomits, until at last his body was almost [over]come by use of poisons to the state of Mithridates's body'.[4] All the while, said Bacon, the duplicitous Carr was writing to Overbury with 'hopes and protestations for his delivery'. The prosecution relied, as it had in previous cases, upon the old rule that the date and time of death were immaterial in a charge of poisoning. As Bacon remarked, 'If in all cases of impoisonment you should require testimony, you should as good proclaim impunity'.

A key plank in the prosecution case consisted of the Northampton/Carr letters (many of them undated like most of the letters referred to in court) which had been found in Sir Robert Cotton's cabinet. These were suspicious in that they identified people by code words, for instance 'Julius' for the King, 'Dominic' for Northampton and 'Unclius' for Canterbury. Unfortunately, many of them were written in a style so cryptic as to render their meaning opaque except to the intended reader. One of Northampton's letters, for example, declared that, 'In this business concerning Overbury there must be a main drift, and a real charge. You may imagine the meaning'. (Bacon suggested that this meant that, while Carr should publicly profess to seek the release of the prisoner, his real aim was to keep him in the Tower.) But there was nothing ambiguous in Northampton's reference to the happy possibility that Overbury might not recover. Carr interrupted Bacon to say that he did not contest the authenticity of the letters or the fact that they referred

---

[4] Mithridates was a King of northern Anatolia who, attempting to kill himself by poison, merely made himself resistant to the drug.

to a plot to get his friend out of the way, simply that they did not prove his part in the murder.

Sir Dudley Digges was then sworn in to tell the court of 'a letter ... from the Lord of Somerset to Overbury that dissuaded him from that course [that is, from accepting the embassy]'. In fact, as Digges made clear, he had not actually seen the letter, merely heard Monson's account of it as related to him by Overbury, such was the lax attitude towards evidence in those days. The Earl flatly denied the implications of the letter, 'I was very willing that he [Overbury] should have undertaken it [that is, the embassy]; but he not'. (After the trial he was to admit that this was a lie.) Bacon then read out the evidence of a number of witnesses, among them the apothecary, Loubell, who claimed that Carr had asked him on a number of occasions about Overbury's state of health. The Earl flatly denied having done so, or that he had seen Loubell more than once.

Turning to Carr's motives, Bacon said that: '(T)here were no mean secrets betwixt my lord and sir T. Overbury that might rather cause him to fear him, than the hindrance of his marriage: if that had been it alone, his going beyond sea would have served the turn'. But Carr, he said, had another reason to fear Overbury. For years the Earl had made him privy to the King's secrets and thus laid himself open to blackmail. He then went meticulously through the documents and admissions which, he said, proved the Earl's guilt. When the prosecutor had finished the Lord High Sheriff, seemingly impressed by the strength of his case, looked up to invite the prisoner to confess his guilt. Carr tersely replied, 'My Lord, I came with a resolution to defend myself'.

The members of the court then took a break to relieve themselves. After they had returned and settled down Serjeant Montague rose to deal with the white powders. Overbury's servant, Payton told how his master had complained to Weston that the powder [seemingly the powder of 5 June 1613] had made him very sick, and had given him in one night '60 stools besides vomits'. (We should not take the number literally; it may simply have been a way of describing a large number in the same way that the number 40 is used in the Bible.) He also told how, when Carr heard that Overbury was very sick from the physic, 'My lord smiled and cried Pish; and so turned him away'. It must have sounded to the jury very much like the reaction of a callous poisoner. Finally, the court was told of Franklin's claim to have seen a letter from Carr to Weston in which he 'wondered whether these things have not yet dispatched'. The letter, he said, went on to warn that Overbury 'was like to come out of the Tower within a few days if Weston did not [ap]ply himself'.

Serjeant Crew was the next to take up the cudgels. After a flowery denunciation of Carr for betraying his friendship with the dead man, he read out a statement of Franklin's describing an occasion when Carr was apparently privy to and secretly participated in an incriminating conversation with Frances:

> 'When my lord of Somerset came to town after Weston's apprehension he (Franklin) was sent for to the Cockpit; and there my lady swore him to secrecy, told him that Weston was taken, and that it was likely he should be so shortly, and that they should all be hanged. Then retiring into an innermost room to speak with one (whom he verily believes to be my lord of Somerset) she came again, and told him that the lords, if they examine him, would put him in hope of a pardon upon confession: But, said she, believe them not; for when they have got out of you what they would, we should all be hanged. Nay, saith Mrs Turner, madam, I will not be hanged for you both.'

Mary Erwin, Mrs Turner's maid confirmed Carr's presence in the house at the time and Crew added that Frances 'confesseth all that Franklin said concerning her discourse with him and that my lord was with her that night'. Carr interrupted vehemently to deny that this meeting had ever taken place.

The prosecutor then turned to Carr's attempts to suppress the evidence against him. Addressing the accused directly, he described how he had obtained a bundle of correspondence by issuing an illegal warrant, and went on:

> 'Now for those letters that passed betwixt my lord of Northampton and you; thirty of those you had sent him, were delivered you after his death by sir R. Cotton; and all these the night before your commitment to the dean of Westminster you burnt. For those letters of Overbury's that you had, sir R. Cotton advised you not to burn, but keep them.'

Carr responded by conceding that he had burnt the letters, but offered no reason for having done so. He also admitted having cut off parts of them 'as impertinent', that is to say, irrelevant: it was hardly a convincing explanation.

Bacon then rose to his feet to deal with the petition for mercy which Carr had addressed to the King in which he confessed to having 'endeavoured the imprisonment of Sir Thomas Overbury', but claimed to have done so only 'for his reformation, not his ruin'. Bacon commented sourly: 'in this Declaration of my lord Somerset there is a brink of confession; I would to God it had a bottom'. As the prosecutor began to recount the statements which the apothecary Loubell had made to the investigators Carr intervened once again to say that he wished that the witness was in court to be examined.

It was at this point that Chief Justice Coke chose to make another of his unwise interventions. In an attempt to explain why Loubell had not been called to give evidence he said, 'It was doubted Loubell might be a delinquent; and therefore I durst not examine him upon oath, no more than I did Franklin, but when in their testimony they accuse themselves, it is as strong as if upon oath'. Long after Coke's day it came to be accepted that statements made by a witness prejudicial to himself were, for the reason he suggests, admissible as an exception to the rule against hearsay but this exception never applied in the trial of a third party. More importantly, by conceding that the evidence of 'a delinquent' was inadmissible unless it amounted to an admission against himself, the judge effectively scuppered a great deal of the prosecution case, much of which was built on the evidence of Franklin and other admitted 'delinquents'. It was a curious *faux pas* from such a distinguished lawyer, but in the end it did not affect the outcome of the trial.

CARR'S DEFENCE

It was seven in the evening when Carr came to reply to the case against him. Amos imaginatively described how, 'The dramatic effect of the scene was increased by a multitude of torches casting a glimmering light through the high and vaulted roofs of the hall and making transiently visible the countenances of the Judges, the Counsellors, the Peers, Peeresses and the mixed audience that crowded the lofty scaffolding'. Everyone was tired, not least the prisoner. '[N]either my memory nor notes will give me leave to answer every particular in order', he grumbled. What follows, therefore, has been re-arranged somewhat to make the Earl's argument clearer.

Carr freely admitted having fallen out with Overbury. '[I]t is', he said, 'no great wonder for friends sometimes to fall out'. Overbury, he suggested, was a particularly rebarbative character, 'I think he had never a friend in his life that he would not sometimes fall out with, and give offence unto: And this they termed insolence in him; but I give it a better name'. The Earl had done all he could, he said, to patch up Overbury's quarrels. When the knight had incurred the Queen's displeasure he had 'laboured his conciliation and return, yet [Overbury] with main terms laid the cause of disgrace upon me'.

Against all the evidence to the contrary – and the admission in his petition for mercy – Carr indignantly denied having persuaded Overbury to refuse the embassy. Indeed, he was 'very willing [Overbury] should undertake it, but he not'. He had an elaborately ingenious explanation of his damning letter urging Overbury not to accept the post:

> 'My lord Canterbury [he said] moved him to it, but not without my privity; for I should have been glad to have removed him, both in respect of my marriage and his insolence. But Overbury came to me, and said, I will tell sir Dudley Diggs [sic] I will undertake this embassage, that he may so return answer to my lord of Canterbury; but then you must write to me not to do so, and so take it upon you.'

The story was less than convincing. Indeed, as Carr was subsequently to confess, it was a lie. He had, he admitted in court, 'consented to [Overbury's] imprisonment', but only 'to the end he should make no impediment in my marriage'. The word 'consented' is an interesting one. By using it, Carr appears to be suggesting that he merely went along with another's plan, presumably Northampton's.

Once Overbury was in the Tower Carr insisted, seemingly with truth, that he had gone out of his way to look after him, 'I had a care of his lodgings, that they should be where he might have the best air, and windows both to the water and within the Tower, so that he might have liberty to speak with whom he would. So you see it was against my intention to have him close prisoner'.

Turning to the question of the State secrets, Carr admitted that he had passed state papers to Overbury, but only for the public good and with royal authority. 'I knew his ability and what I did was by the King's Commission'. Bacon had no quarrel with this: his argument was that the sharing of secrets had laid Carr open to blackmail. But it was a weak point, since the prosecution produced no evidence, did not even suggest, that Overbury had ever hinted at blackmailing his patron.

Dealing with the 'powder', Carr admitted that he had sent it to Carr in the Tower, but only, 'so I might have the better occasion to speak for him to the King for that purpose, he himself desired it'. He also had an answer to the accusation that he had sent in poisoned tarts, 'Whereas it is pretended that I should cause poisoned tarts to be sent him to the Tower; my wife in her confession saith, That there were none sent but either by me or her; and some were wholesome, and some not: Then it must needs follow, that the good ones were those which I sent, and the bad hers'. The logic was impeccable, but Bacon attempted to discredit it by reference to the terms of an undated letter which the Countess had written to Elwes. Like much of Frances' writing, the language is cryptic and its meaning was to be strongly disputed. The relevant part read, 'I was bid to bid you say, that these tarts came not from me; and again, I was bid to tell you, that you must take heed of the tarts, because there be letters in them, and therefore neither give your wife nor children of them, but of the wine you may, for there are no letters in it'.

An endorsement on the letter in Bacon's handwriting declares that Frances had admitted that the word 'letters' was code for poison, but, as the historian, Gardiner suggested, it is more probable that 'the tarts went backwards and forwards as media of a correspondence, and that Elwes invented the theory of the poison in order to conceal his breach of trust in permitting it to go on through his hands, and to magnify his own merits in stopping the poison from arriving'.[5]

---

[5] Samuel R. Gardiner, *History of England from the Accession of James I to the Outbreak of the Civil War, 1603–1642,* Vol. 2 (London, Longman, Green and Co, 1883). And see also Winwood's record of the trial discussed below.

One of the judges asked Carr who it was could 'bid' his wife except himself? Before he could reply Serjeant Montague interjected, 'The continual letters between my lord and her argues that'. Instead of answering the question Carr recapitulated his position. 'But for Overbury, my furthest intent in his imprisonment was, that he should be no impediment to my marriage; and this I communicated to my Lord of Northampton and Elwes'. Montague responded bitterly and ungrammatically, 'You could not couple yourself worse than with them two'. It was an unenlightening exchange which failed to resolve any of the issues raised by the letter.

Carr's explanation of his re-dating of the Northampton letters was unconvincing. It was done, he claimed, at Cotton's urging 'on the ground that they might prove useful to me at this time'. He added ruefully, 'I wish that my answers to those letters were now to be seen; and if I had ever thought that those letters of my Lord of Northampton's would be dangerous to me, it is likely I would never have kept them'. (He seems to have overlooked the implications of this statement on his motives for burning the other letters.) He went on to express a wish that Cotton were present 'to clear many things that now be obscure'. At this, Bacon jumped in to remind everyone of the court's dubious ruling that, even if Cotton were present 'he could not be sworn for reasons of state, being held as a delinquent'.

The accused made no attempt to justify his illegal warrant, but sought once again to shift the blame onto others:

> '[M]y wife desired me to do it for Mrs. Turner's sake; [his secretary] Packer formed it [that is, drafted the warrant], and told me I might do it as a [Privy] Councillor alone, without other hands; for I would have had at that time my Lord Knowles to have joined with me, but that he was at Council'. At this, the Lord Chancellor dryly observed, 'All the Council together could not justify the making of such a warrant.'

Carr went on to protest that he had been moved to seek a pardon because of the risks posed by the grave affairs of State with which he had been dealing, '[H]aving had many things of trust under the King, and the custody of both the seals, without particular warrant, I desired by this means to be exonerated'. He blamed Cotton for the wide terms of the second draft. His friend had urged that, 'In respect you have received some disgrace in the opinion of the world, in having past that pardon which the last summer you desired, especially seeing there be many precedents of larger, I would have you now get one after the largest precedent, that so by that addition you might recover your honour'. An incriminating reference in the draft to 'mercy' had been suggested, Carr claimed, by Elwes. His attempts to shift the blame for each of his actions must have seemed particularly unattractive to the court.

At the end of the prisoner's defence the Lord High Sheriff gushingly declared that the Earl had 'behaved himself modestly and wittily' in court and went on to invite him to follow his wife's example by pleading guilty. Carr ignored the offer and made one last desperate plea to his peers, 'As the King hath raised me to your degree, so he hath now disposed me to your censures. This may be any of your own cases, and therefore I assure myself you will not take circumstances for evidence; for if you should, the condition of a man's life were nothing'. After Carr's hour-long defence, the court retired to consider their verdict.

CONVICTION AND SENTENCE

When they returned, each member of the court delivered his judgment one by one, bareheaded and with his hand on his heart: it was a unanimous verdict of guilty. Asked whether he had anything to say, Carr, who had by then removed his George, began a plea for a death according to his degree, that is to say, by beheading instead of hanging. He was cut short in this by the court and, like his wife before him, sentenced to be hanged, but without the hint of mercy which had been held out to her. The Lord Steward broke his staff of office and the trial was over.

But not the humiliation.

As a felon, Carr's land and possessions were automatically forfeit to the Crown, and the royal officials were determined to get every last piece of it. Oldisworth wrote of their inventory in mouth-licking terms which anticipate the language of today's popular press:

> 'We read of bedsteads with gilt pillars, and purple velvet furniture; of large Persian, Turkey, and Egyptian carpets; of pavilions of cobweb lawn, embroidered with silk flowers; of tapestries representing the wars of Troy and Roman story; of many pictures, described as "great tables," and whole-length portraits. The jewels and plate with which they embellished their courtly lives were of a splendour which might well have lit the spark of jealousy even in a royal breast, and it is easy to imagine what was their destiny.'

The rhymesters too had a field day:

> 'Thou wast a man but of compounded part;
> Nothing thy own but thy aspiring heart.
> Thy house Raleigh's, Westmoreland's thy land,
> Overbury's thy wit, Essex' thy wife. So stand
> By Aesop's law, each bird may pluck his feather,
> And thou stript naked art to wind and weather.
> Yet care of friends, to shelter thee from cold.
> Have mewed thee up in London's strongest hold.
> Summer is set, and winter is come on,
> Yet Robin Redbreast's chirping voice is gone.'

The Queen was delighted with the outcome and presented Coke with a precious ring for his services (to justice, we must hope). James was mightily relieved that the Earl had gone relatively quietly to his fate; after a stressful time he could now relax and enjoy undisturbed the charms of his new Favourite. Three months

The Somersets on Trial

later, Villiers was created Baron Whaddon of Whaddon and Viscount Villiers. In January of the following year the young man was elevated to the Earldom of Buckingham, and the next month sworn in as a member of the Privy Council. Just under a year later he was created a Marquess, the highest rank of the nobility short of a Duke. So extraordinary was this succession of preferments that James felt it necessary to justify them to the Lords with what, for its age, was an amazingly frank defence of homosexual love:

> 'I, James, am neither God nor an angel, but a man like any other. Therefore I act like a man, and confess to loving those dear to me more than other men. You may be sure that I love the Earl of Buckingham more than anyone else, and more than you who are here assembled. I wish to speak in my own behalf, and not to have it thought to be a defect, for Jesus Christ did the same, and therefore I cannot be blamed. Christ had his John, and I have my George.'

It takes a certain amount of *chutzpah* to compare oneself to the Son of God, though perhaps different standards apply to God's anointed.

ACT 10

WAS JUSTICE DONE?

James lived up to his promise by granting Frances a pardon almost immediately after her conviction, not a full pardon, because she had to remain in the Tower, but a pardon which lifted the sentence of death from her.[1] He had done so, the pardon declared, out of the 'divers and manifold causes of our clemency', including her 'noble progeny', the fact that she was merely an accessory, that she had freely confessed and sought mercy, that the peers had interceded on her behalf, and that she had been influenced by 'certain base persons', presumably Anne Turner and her coven of magicians, thugs and fantasists.

Her husband's pardon was to take much longer to arrive. Nevertheless, two months after the trial Lord Hay was despatched to bring Carr a message of comfort: the King intended to do whatever he could 'to repair him again, to restore his liberty and his honour and eventually to pardon him'. Soon after, the prisoners were granted the liberty of the Tower and permitted to live in adjoining rooms. Rumours of a second pregnancy followed, but whether true or not, no child resulted. Contrary to all precedent, Carr was at no stage removed from the Order of the Garter and

---

[1] Sir Simonds D'Ewes claims that the pardon was the result of the 'earnest and daily intercession' of Frances' father, still Lord Treasurer, and Queen Anne.

was allowed to wear the George even in custody. Emboldened by these signs of favour, he sought recovery of his property. James responded by offering him a settlement worth £7,000 a year, only to have it rejected outright. Carr insisted on nothing less than the return of his estates in full. Unfortunately for him, most of these had already been disposed of to others. After much negotiation the Earl agreed, in exchange for a settlement on his daughter, to accept an annual allowance of £4,000 and restoration to the barony of Winwick. It was an outcome less generous than had originally been offered.

Eventually, in January 1622, some six years after their convictions, James permitted the Somersets to leave the Tower and retire. They were given the choice of two country houses, but forbidden to stray further than three miles from their boundaries. They chose Lord Wallingford's home, Rotherfield Grays in Oxfordshire. Two years later, Carr received his pardon. It was in less generous terms than his wife's and required him not to resume his seat in the House of Lords. One can only wonder whether the King ever reflected upon his solemn pledge that anyone who spared Overbury's murderer should be cursed for eternity.

Relations between the couple grew strained over the years and they lived in separate wings of the building. Gossip had it that they had come to loathe each other and never exchanged a friendly greeting again, but in truth little is known of their intimate relations. In August 1632 Frances, then living with her husband at Chiswick, died of breast cancer and either ovarian or uterine cancer. Warped misogynists like Wilson rejoiced in this as poetic justice for someone who had allowed lust to rule her life.

In time, Buckingham started to become an embarrassment to James. Some say that this moved him to resume his correspondence with the Earl on almost a weekly basis. Whether there was truth in this or not, there came a time when Carr thought it propitious to seek restoration of the remainder of his property; but he had left it too late. James died at Theobalds on 27 March 1625. His son and successor, Charles, had no time for the scandal-ridden Earl, who after leaving the Tower had twice been suspected of financial improprieties. Finally, on 17 July 1645, two decades after James' death, Carr died, as *The State Trials* report put it, 'in obscurity'.

Before arriving at a judgement on the character and conduct of this proud, foolish man we should first consider whether he had received a fair trial.

DID THE EARL HAVE A FAIR TRIAL?

Carr had borne the ordeal of his trial bravely but not skillfully. As he wrote in a letter to the King shortly afterwards, 'I fell rather for want of well defending, than by the violence of force of any proofs'. It was a judgement with which Secretary Winwood agreed, 'Never man spake more poorly for himself'. But was the trial fair? The cynical Weldon had no doubt that it had been fixed:

> 'And now the game to be plaid, in which Somerset must be the loser, the cards being cut, and dealt between the King and sir Edward Cook, chief justice, whose daughter Purbeck, Villiers had married or was to marry, and therefore a fit instrument to ruine Somerset and secretary Wynwood. These all played: the stake; Somerset's life and his lady's, and their fortune, and the family of Suffolk: some of them played booty [dishonestly], and in truth the game was not plaid above-board.'

Was he right in this? Most of what we know comes from *The State Trials* reports. These are curious records to modern eyes, interspersed as they are with quotations of varying reliability from other sources. Nor can we rule out the possibility that they were biassed. Professor Amos put the point well:

> 'We should not attach much credit to a report published by the Austrian Government of a trial of William Tell, or, by the French Republic of the trials of Louis XVI and of Queen Marie Antoi-

nette; but, in our domestic history, we are too apt to surrender our belief to the only extant details of our ancient State Trials, without duly considering by whom and with what motives they were published.'

Fortunately, we have another (partial) record of Carr's trial to compare with that in *The State Trials*. It was found among the archives of the State Paper Office and appears to have been in the handwriting of Sir Ralph Winwood. The differences between the two accounts were meticulously spelled out in *The Great Oyer*. As an example of the many revealing discrepancies, Amos points to the fact that the official report contains no reference to a letter referred to by Serjeant Crew in which, Winwood tells us, 'Overbury writ to Somerset that the powder had wrought well with him, &c., but that he meant to take no more'. It was an important confirmation of Carr's explanation of his motives in sending the powder to the prisoner. Also missing in the official report was any reference to the fact recorded by Winwood that Loubell the apothecary had told his investigators that Carr 'willed him to write to Dr Maiot concerning physic to be given to Overbury'.[2] More significantly, the printed report omits a vital 'perhaps' when quoting Frances' admission that the word, 'letters' referred to poison. As to the relative reliability of the two records, Amos suggests that Bacon's speech in the printed report is more polished, whereas Carr's defence as recorded by Winwood reads more life-like. It is certainly curious that wherever *The State Trials* report differs from Winwood's note the latter usually leans towards the Earl's innocence, despite the fact that its author was no friend of his.

---

[2] The 'Maiot' referred to in the letter is usually presumed to be Dr Mayerne. However, it has been pointed out that there was another physician of a similar name in London at this time, the German alchemist Michael Maier (Ron Heisler, 'Michael Maier and England', *The Hermetic Journal*, 1989). Mayerne customarily signed himself 'Mayernus', whereas Michael Maier used the name, 'Mayerus'.

Passion, Poison and Power

What is certain is that the court which tried the Earl was not the impartial tribunal we would expect today. The seven Commissioners on the bench included three of the accused's most bitter enemies, as well as the Lord Chief Justice, who was thus at various times investigator, prosecutor and judge in the same case. (At one point Coke the judge actually defended the actions of Coke the investigator.) And the Lord High Steward's only interventions in the proceedings consisted of exhortations to the accused to make a full confession, even at the point when he was just about to begin his defence.

Before the trial began, the Somersets had been put under enormous pressure to confess. High dignitaries had been sent to them, sometimes secretly at night, with offers of mercy should they agree to plead guilty, yet no one told the court of this or the fact that Carr had refused to cave in over so long a period of time. Despite a hint to the contrary in *The Great Oyer*, there is no evidence that torture was employed in any of the Overbury investigations, notwithstanding that both Coke and Bacon were no strangers to such practices.[3] Nevertheless, it would be foolish to ignore the fact that witnesses must have been fearful of what could have been done to them should they have refused to cooperate with their interrogators.

But if Bacon did not resort to torture he was certainly not above trickery. Amos set out clearly how:

> '... by the artful selection of passages and detaching them from their context or other explanatory or contradictory matter, a confession, deposition, letter, or other paper was often made to appear to have a totally different import from what really belonged to it,

---

[3] Contemporary tortures included the Manacles, by which the prisoner could be hung from the wall, Little Ease, a four foot high cage in which he could be confined, and most feared of all, the rack, a single application of which could leave a man – or woman – permanently without the use of their limbs.

and to obtain credit which no one reading the entire document would think it deserved. This process of garbling evidence was, in effect, equivalent to manufacturing it.'

Elwes was even bold enough to complain at his trial about the Attorney's practice of reading out selective, even garbled, extracts of his statements and documents, 'You have paraphrased upon every examination. You have aggravated every evidence and applied it to me, so that I stand clearly condemned before I am found guilty'.

The conduct of a criminal trial in Coke's day bears only a passing resemblance to contemporary practice. The accused was not given warning of the charges against him. When Carr asked the court for advance notice of them he was told that such a process did not 'stand with the course of justice'. He was denied the right to be represented by counsel and the right to call witnesses on his own behalf. Nor was he was allowed to cross-examine the witnesses who were called against him. The idea that the burden of proof lies on the prosecution to prove their case, so important in our eyes today, was not to emerge for another couple of centuries: in Bacon's time there was actually a presumption in favour of the Crown in the sense that an acquittal on indictment was considered almost an affront to His Majesty; they were not called the King's courts for nothing.

A particular injustice, at least to modern eyes, was the extent to which the prosecution were permitted to use hearsay, that is to say evidence of what the witness was told by someone else. Hearsay, by definition, consists of statements not taken under oath. Even in the seventeenth century it was beginning to be realized that such statements needed to be viewed with caution. The reason for this is that the original speaker cannot be subject to cross-examination, the process in our system of justice by which evidence is tested. The confessions of Franklin, Weston and Elwes were among the most incriminating evidence against the Earl, yet all three of

Passion, Poison and Power

these 'witnesses' were dead and in their graves at the time of his trial. Even double hearsay was allowed, that is to say, hearsay of hearsay. A case in point was Sir Dudley Digges who was allowed to tell the court the contents of an incriminating letter which he knew of only from what he had been told by Sir Robert Mansell. Even more remarkably, when documents were quoted in court they were never produced for the court to examine. Franklin was said to have made three confessions, yet not one of them was shown to a court and none of the summaries which were offered in their stead was identical to either of the others.

Finally, the prosecution was allowed to get away with what even then were highly dubious presumptions of law. Bacon, for example, was allowed to assert without contradiction the proposition that the manner of Overbury's death could not be disputed because it had been determined in another trial, '[A]ll the world by law is concluded to say', he claimed erroneously, 'that Overbury was poisoned by Weston'. Serjeant Montague repeated this error when he told the court, 'Four several juries have found this white powder was poison and of this poison Sir Thomas Overbury died'. Even had this been the case (which it was not) it was a wholly unjust inference. Carr had played no part in Weston's trial; he had had no opportunity to cross-examine the witnesses in that case, and the court's conclusions were not legally binding upon him in his own trial.[4] Equally objectionable was the way in which witnesses were allowed to give their opinions on the very issues which the court had to decide. The most blatant example of this was Franklin's statement that 'he dares take his oath (that) the Earl was guilty'.

Perhaps the most obviously unappealing aspect of Carr's trial was the way in which the Somersets' reputation had been publicly besmirched even before they had been accused of any crime.

---

[4] It was not until the reign of George III that this point was clarified.

Weston's prosecutor was instructed publicly – for no good reason at law – to set out the facts 'without sparing any of [those involved] or omitting anything material against them'. It was a stratagem blatantly directed at the Somersets, and it was resorted to in one form or another throughout the remaining trials.

It would be wrong to suggest that the outcome of Carr's trial was a foregone conclusion in the sense that a finding of guilty was inevitable: you only have to read the correspondence between Bacon and the King to realize that. Nor was the trial corrupt in the sense that the prosecution were cynically attempting to secure the conviction of someone they believed to be innocent – to the contrary, they seem to have had no doubt of his guilt – but the process was nevertheless far from fair. Carr's trial was probably no less just than others of its day, but that only means that it was pretty unjust. But did the verdict of the court get to the truth of the matter? In other words and putting legal quibbles aside, was Carr actually a party to the murder of his one time friend?

ACT 11

WAS CARR A MURDERER?

In a letter to the King shortly before the trial began, Bacon candidly acknowledged that the proof of the Earl's guilt rested 'chiefly on presumptions' and begged him not to 'take circumstances for evidence'. (Carr was to make exactly this plea to the peers at his trial.) In fact, circumstantial evidence, if clear enough, can be the strongest of proofs, but was that the case with Carr?

No matter how you cut it, Robert Carr was the most obvious candidate for Overbury's murderer. Enraged and frustrated at his friend's hostility to the annulment he so strongly desired and grossly offended at the vilification of his intended bride, he had fallen in with Northampton's plot to trick his former friend into the Tower, where he was to meet his death. And when his involvement came to light he did everything he in his power to avoid being prosecuted, even to the point of illegality. Who could not suspect him? But suspicion is not enough: where is the evidence that he brought about or even intended his old friend's death?

It is certainly true that Carr lied to the court about urging Overbury to reject the embassy; admitted as much after he had been convicted. It follows that the tortuous explanation for his actions which he gave at his trial was a fabrication. Suspicious? Yes, but not conclusive of guilt. Innocent people on trial for their life will often lie if they think it will secure their acquittal. In any event, Carr neatly sidestepped the implications of his conduct by what the lawyers call a confession and avoidance: he *had* been part of a plot, but only with a view to compelling Overbury to withdraw his objections to the proposed marriage and not in order to have him killed. The very discreditability of this motive makes it all the more persuasive.

Two witnesses spoke of Carr's fear of what might happen if Overbury were allowed to live. John Simcocks, described by one commentator as 'a man of some fashion and good understanding', disclosed how his friend, Weston, 'many times ... told him that my Lord of Somerset charged him to look to Overbury well; for if ever he came out, one of us two must die for it'. Franklin sang a similar tune when he claimed to have seen a letter from Carr warning that if Overbury were to come out of the Tower in two days 'they all should be undone'. But Simcocks' statement might simply have meant that the two men were so much at odds that, when the prisoner was released they feared he might take revenge on his tormentor. Franklin's use of the word, 'undone' might likewise have referred to nothing more than disclosure of the plot to have Overbury imprisoned.

There was, it is true, Franklin's claim that Frances had told him she had received a letter from Carr saying that he '[marvelled] at these delays, that the business is not dispatched'. At the Earl's trial he claimed that these words referred to something other than Overbury's murder. Despite his failure to elaborate on this explanation the fact is that it was never disproved. Furthermore, a sharp-eyed commentator has pointed out that, although no date is given for the letter in the printed report, in the manuscript, it is referred to as 'about a month after Whitsuntide'. Whitsuntide fell on 4 April that year and Overbury died about three months later, which seems to bear out Carr's explanation.[1]

Seemingly more incriminating was Franklin's account, described above, of the supposed meeting of the 'poisoners' at which Carr was said to have been a concealed participant. The Earl hotly denied the story and offered a convincing objection to it. 'If Franklin knew me so well, and that I was privy to the plot, why should then my wife and I, (as he pretends,) when he was there, speak so closely, and always out of his hearing and sight?'. Franklin was a known liar. As the Earl said to the court, 'I do not think you can take (him) for a good witness'. Even Coke privately described the man as a 'foul' witness.

The prosecution relied heavily on the Northampton letters, particularly on one of them in which the writer referred to Carr having 'prompted the Lieutenant', but the Earl had a plausible explanation for this too. He 'conceive[d] [Northampton's] meaning to be, that he should endeavour to make Overbury be a good instrument betwixt my Lord of Suffolk and me'. In other words, the writer was referring only to the plot to pressure Overbury into withdrawing his objection to Frances' annulment and not to any intent to murder.

Carr's efforts to destroy the letters were certainly suspicious. He tried to argue that they would have taken on an entirely different meaning if only his replies had been saved along with them: it was a safe claim to make for he knew that they no longer existed. And his explanation for having destroyed some of the letters hardly squares with his feverish efforts to find them in the first place. But in assessing Carr's conduct we should consider

---

[1] As pointed out in an Appendix to the so-called *Bacon's Dictionary* (George E. Ellis, *Bacon's Dictionary of Boston with an Historical Introduction* (Boston and New York, Houghton Mifflin and Co., 1886)).

the state of mind he must have been in when he became aware that he was suspected of murder. Even by his own account he had behaved dishonourably towards his old friend and must have realized that when this came out he would inevitably fall under suspicion. But there may have been other reasons for the bonfire of the letters quite unconnected with Overbury's death which Carr would not have wished to disclose even when on trial for his life, notably his secret negotiations with Spain. (Although he denied it vigorously to the Commissioners, it now seems likely that the Earl was actually receiving a pension from England's old enemy.) He must have realized that his conduct could easily be construed as treasonable.

But why should an innocent man apply for a pardon in the first place? Carr explained it as a normal precaution for someone who had exercised great functions of State; and, indeed, there were precedents for such applications. Serjeant Crew saw it as sinister that, instead of the greatest offences being listed first in the draft, they had been buried in the body of the document. The Earl's response was to blame the lawyers, who had fashioned the draft in the widest terms 'without [his] privity'. Like his other attempts to shift blame, it was not an attractive defence, but it was one which the prosecution were unable to disprove. (They could, after all, have called Cotton to give evidence on the point.)

Much play was made at the Earl's trial of his supposed role in sending poisoned food to the prisoner. Once more, he had an irrefutable explanation – since he had not sent any it must have come from Frances – an explanation which both Weston and Elwes seemed to confirm. Even Elwes agreed that the food sent by Carr had been 'counterfeited' by the poisoners. Bacon sought to parry this argument by pointing to Frances' statement that she had been 'bid to bid you' to say that the poisoned tarts had not come from her. The judges seemed to have agreed that it was unlikely that anyone other than her husband could have 'bidden', that is instructed, her

Passion, Poison and Power

in this matter. At one stage the court was told that Frances had admitted that the 'bidder' was her husband. However, as we have seen, Winwood heard a 'perhaps' in the Countess's statement, which greatly reduces its value. Later, when asked about it in the Tower, Frances claimed that the 'bidder' was 'Northampton or Weston, not pitching upon certainty'.[2] The judges' presumption was unwarranted, as even the King agreed.

Serjeant Montague placed great stress on the fact that Carr had sent powders to Overbury, but was unable to produce any evidence to counter the Earl's explanation, backed up by firm evidence including a letter from the dead man, that they had been sent at the prisoner's own request in a bid to attract the King's sympathy. We should also note Carr's frankness in freely admitting to the commission his sending in of the powder. As the historian, Samuel R. Gardiner, commented, 'It is, to say the least of it, extremely improbable that, if [Carr] intended to poison Overbury, he would bring suspicion upon himself by sending him harmless medicines at the same time'.[3] That of course does not overcome the fact that the prisoner suffered abominably from the powder which Carr had sent to him on 5 June 1613. There could be other explanations for this; the apothecary who prepared the powder might have upped the dose when the previous powders had failed, or Overbury might have been a victim of simple food poisoning, a condition far from rare even today.

To look at the other side of the coin, anyone seeking to establish Carr's guilt must be able to explain why, if he was determined to murder Overbury, he should have gone to the length of setting up a complex plot to have him locked up? Could he not as easily

---

[2] Bacon's letter to Villiers of 2 May 1616.
[3] Samuel R. Gardiner, *History of England from the Accession of James I to the Outbreak of the Civil War, 1603–1642,* Vol. 2 (London, Longman, Green and Co, 1883).

have been poisoned at home? And why if someone wished to kill the prisoner would they subject him to otherwise pointless months of pressure to change his mind over the matter of the annulment? We have no reason to doubt Carr's claim to have done his best to obtain tolerable conditions for his friend while in the Tower. And there is firm evidence that he sought medical assistance for him. But perhaps the strongest point in the Earl's favour was Frances' consistent protestations of his innocence. When a wife pleads guilty to murder, questions inevitably arise about her husband's involvement in the crime, but from beginning to end Frances refused resolutely to incriminate her Robert, even when under great pressure and at a time when it was in her interests to do so.

Not being burdened by the constraints of the law, we are able to take note of otherwise inadmissible material. There is an archive of the More family known as the Losely Papers, which consists mostly of holograph letters from King James to Sir George More, Elwes' successor at the Tower. Among them is an unsigned memorandum which reads, 'I have often talked with Mr James, [Carr's] chief servant, about (the accusation of murder), who ever was of opinion that My lord was clear, and his Lady only guilty, for one time Mrs. Turner told him, that little did My lord know what she had adventured for his Lady: but the truth is, King James was weary of him: Buckingham had supplied his place'. Goodness knows, this anonymous scribbling is worth little, but its general thrust at least points in the same direction as Carr's own story.

Perhaps the most convincing judgement on Carr's involvement in Overbury's death was that of Weldon, 'Many believe the Earl of Somerset guilty of Overbury's death, but they most thought him guilty only of the breach of friendship (and that in a high point) by suffering his imprisonment, which was the highway to his murder; and this conjecture I take to be of the soundest opinion'. This conclusion accords well with Carr's determination not to plead Guilty to murder even in the face of intolerable pressure from the man who held his life in his hands. If that is a correct assessment then the Earl's reply to Bacon, when offered mercy in exchange for a plea of guilty, takes on a measure of nobility, 'Life and fortune are not worth the acceptance, when honour is gone'.

But if not Carr, then, who or what killed Overbury? There were some very strange theories going around.

ACT 12

THE CONSPIRACY THEORIES

Coke's suspicions of a widespread Popish plot were in tune with the prevailing dread of England's old enemy, Catholic Spain. At the time of Monson's abortive trial, the Tuscan ambassador reported to his master that the Privy Council could think of nothing else. One of the side effects of this panic was speculation that there were others in the plot to murder Overbury, possibly persons of quality and influence, who had not been brought to trial.

Franklin was one of the foremost begetters of these rumours. He told the divines sent to hear his confession that Frances' father, Thomas Howard, was involved, adding sinisterly, 'I could discover [that is, reveal] Knights, great men and others. I am almost ashamed to speak what I know'. He offered to make 'one discovery that should deserve my life'. Even on the scaffold, after a piece of clowning which involved trying to put the rope about the hangman's neck, he declared that, as well as Carr, 'there were three greater birds and Lords ... than yet discovered'. Onlookers thought him mad or drunk, either or both of which may have been the case. Franklin was a known liar prepared to say anything that would put off his demise and little reliance can be placed on his words, but could there have been an element of truth behind them?

DID JAMES HAVE A HIDDEN AGENDA?

No one can read the story of Overbury's fall without noticing how much the King was involved at every stage. He had been the promoter of Essex' marriage to Frances; when that went wrong he had supported and facilitated, even to the extent of impropriety, the annulment which Overbury so bitterly opposed. The attempt to get Overbury out of the country by the offer of an embassy, if not actually initiated by James, could only have been made with his consent. As one contemporary wrote:

> 'It is conceived that the King hath a good while been much distasted with the said gentleman, even in his own nature, for too stiff a carriage of his fortune; besides that scandalous offence of the Queen at Greenwich, which was never but a palliated cure. Upon which considerations his majesty resolving to sever him from my Lord of Rochester, and to do it not disgracefully nor violently, but in some honourable fashion, commanded not long since the archbishop by way of familiar discourse to propound unto him the embassage of France or of the Arch-Duke's court, whereof the one was shortly to be changed, and the other, at the present, vacant.'[1]

There is no evidence that James countenanced Overbury's being set up to refuse the offer of an embassy, but was the King, as some have suggested, ill disposed toward the Earl as a result of his discovery of a new love? Sir Simonds D'Ewes wrote of James 'having at that time fixed his eyes upon the delicate personage and features of Mr George Villiers, he was the more easily induced to suffer the Earl of Somerset to be removed from his court and presence, to the Tower of London'. This almost certainly goes too far. While there was undoubtedly a sea change in James' affections when Villiers appeared on the scene, all the evidence points to his

---

[1] Letter of 22 April 1613 from Sir H. Wotton to Sir Edmund Bacon, quoted by Edward Rimbault, Ll.D., in Edward F. Rimbault, Ll.D. (ed.), *The Miscellaneous Works in Prose and Verse of Sir Thomas Overbury Knt., Now First Collected* (London, John Russell Smith, 1856).

The Conspiracy Theories

continuing to treat Carr in a kindly, even generous manner, which is why he was so put our when he experienced the former Favourite's bitterness. As James Spedding, the nineteenth-century editor of Bacon's works, observed, James' lengthy letter rebuking the Earl for his behaviour (quoted above) was not in 'the language of an affection wearied of itself and seeking occasion to escape from its bonds, but of one painfully alive, passionately loyal, bitterly resenting the inadequacy of the affection with which it is requited, and earnestly desiring to be restored to its former condition'.

Others had darker suspicions. While Overbury was lying in the Tower the Earl of Southampton wrote to Winwood declaring that a 'rooted hatred lyeth in the King's heart towards [Overbury]'.[2] There is some slender evidence for this. Three weeks after his son had been arrested, Overbury senior petitioned the King for the lifting of the close confinement in which he was being kept: the request was denied. The prosecution at Carr's trial blamed the Earl for Overbury's treatment in the Tower; in fact it was James himself who was responsible, as he himself confirmed. In a letter of 29 December 1615 he referred to the 'case of Overbury, who was committed to the Tower, and there kept a close prisoner *by my comaundment*'[3] (emphasis added).

Amos lent support to this picture of a vindictive King when he claimed that James had a malicious streak, as evidenced by his treatment of Lady Arbella Stuart who at the time of Overbury's death was, in his words, 'expiring in another chamber [of the Tower] ... the victim of [James'] groundless suspicion'. In fact, Arbella's case was by no means as straightforward as this: she had a colourable claim to the English throne and could therefore be

---

[2] Quoted in Andrew Amos, *The Great Oyer of Poisoning: The Trial of the Earl of Somerset for the possible poisoning of Sir Thomas Overbury* (London, Richard Bentley, 1846).
[3] *Archeologia*.

Passion, Poison and Power

considered a possible threat to the incumbent. When in 1610 she secretly married another potential claimant, she was thrown into the Tower, from which she made an audacious escape. Caught at sea and returned to captivity, Arbella gradually lost her reason and eventually starved herself to death. Her fate may have been cruel, but it was not one which shows James in an unduly unfavourable light, given the attitudes of the time.

Even when added together, these tidbits form a slender rope on which to hang a cat, let alone a King. Nevertheless, James was undoubtedly fearful that Carr might reveal something concerning himself. A few weeks after his conviction the Earl wrote a long, rambling, almost incoherent letter to James begging for mercy. It hinted at a mutual secret when it referred to 'the acts of your mercy which are not communicable, nor the causes of them with others; as derived from those secret motives which are only sensible and privy to your own heart, and admit of no search or discovery to any general satisfaction'. What *did* he mean?

WAS MURDER THE KING'S DARK SECRET?

The State Trials reported a rumour of 'Somerset's threatening message sent to King James by the Lieutenant of the Tower that if he had not his pardon he should discover [that is, reveal] an important secret which it was the king's interest to have concealed'. There is clear evidence that as the day of Carr's trial approached, James became increasingly agitated. When the Earl was arraigned it was reported that 'His Majesty was so extreme dad[4] and discontented, as he did retire himself from all company, and did forbear both dinner and supper, nothing giving him contentment, until he had

---

[4] An old Scottish term for 'knocked'.

The Conspiracy Theories

heard what answer the Earl had made. It showed something was feared would in passion have broken from him'.[5]

On the day of the trial he was in an even worse state:

> '... who[ever] had seen the King's restless motion all that day, sending to every boat he saw landing at the bridge, cursing all that came without tidings, would have easily judged all was not right, and there had been some grounds for his fear of Somerset's boldness [that is to say, his fear that Somerset would make embarrassing revelations in court]; but at last one bringing him word he was condemned ... All was quiet.'[6]

In a letter dated May 1616, James wrote – in his own hand it should be noted – 'it is easy to be seen, that [Carr] would threaten me with laying an aspersion upon me of being in some sort accessory to his crime [that is, the murder of Overbury]'.

As with so much in the Overbury story, there is plenty of suspicion, but little in the way of proof. In the end it was the historian, Spedding, who put his finger on the weakness in the notion that the King was determined to hush up some scandal:

> 'Had [the King] been afraid of provoking him [Carr], he might easily, keeping the inquiry close and in his own hands, have managed it so as to keep him in temper by secretly favouring or promising to favour him. What does he do? He leaves it all to Sir Edward Coke the most unsubservient, intractable, self-willed, contradictious, and indiscreet man in his dominions, a man whose pride was in his reputation for probity and independence, and who was as staunch as a bloodhound in hunting out evidence; leaves it to him without any restriction upon his discretion, or any watch kept over him; puts the probe into his hands without any caution

---

[5] Mr Sherborne to Sir D. Carleton, 31 May 1616, quoted in Bouchier's *Lives and Letters*.
[6] Sir George More's comment, as reported in Sir Anthony Weldon (attrib.), *The Court and Character of King James I* (1650).

except a solemn injunction, as he would avoid God's curse, to search it to the bottom.'[7]

An eighteenth-century historian spoke for many when he conjectured that the secret of which the King feared disclosure 'was the revealing of that vice to which James seems to have been addicted, that was the object of his fear'.[8] We shall never know, but no one, least of all a king, would want the grubby details of a former relationship, however, trivial, to be the subject of common gossip.

THE MEDICAL MEN

A number of commentators have drawn attention to the suspicious role of James' personal physician. Dr Mayerne was as close to the King as anyone, even sometimes acting as his confidential agent in non-medical matters. At James' request he had treated Overbury in the Tower, and it is hard to believe that the two of them did not from time to time discuss the deteriorating state of the prisoner's health.

There are a number of loose ends surrounding the roles of Mayerne. Rimbault, the editor of Overbury's *Works*, expressed a popular view when he described the doctor as 'the prime mover in the secret state poisonings of the English capital'. Certainly people have asked why Mayerne was not questioned at the outset of the investigation as the King directed. Perhaps he was, but the record has simply not survived? Perhaps his evidence was judged unhelpful? Perhaps the King trusted his adviser too much? A greater mystery is why neither Mayerne nor the coroner were called to give evidence as to the cause of Overbury's death. We

---

[7] *Archeologia.*
[8] William Harris, *An Historical and Critical Account of the Life and Writings of James the First* (London, W. Strahan et al, 1752).

may speculate that the King would not wish his close friend to be laid open to public questioning on this sensitive matter, but we will probably never know what was in his mind.

And then there was Mayerne's dispenser, Paul de Loubell. An intriguing story came to light during the examination of Edward Rider, the landlord of Loubell's father. One day when Rider was collecting the rent he came across the father, who told him that Overbury had not been poisoned, but had 'died of a consumption [an old term for pulmonary tuberculosis] proceeding of a melancholy, by reason of his imprisonment, speaking very hardly against those that went about to prove Sir Thomas to be poisoned'. A week later Rider met the man again, this time accompanied by his wife. Without disclosing that he knew it was Loubell junior's boy who had administered the clyster, Rider casually remarked that he had heard that Overbury had been poisoned by an apothecary's son who had since run away. According to Rider, Loubell's wife then said to her husband in French, 'Oh! husband, That was William you sent into France', or words to that effect. Loubell senior looked at his wife and 'his teeth did chatter as if he trembled'. He went on to tell Rider that he had sent the boy with a letter to Paris, but did not know why he had subsequently left his master. It was a suspicious reaction, but one which might be explained by simple fear of the conclusions which others might draw from the conversation. Nevertheless, it is difficult to understand why it seems never to have been followed up.

A few years earlier, court gossip had been more concerned at the death of an even more prominent person.

THE 'SWEET BABE'S DEATH

Shortly after the heir apparent, Prince Henry, had died in 1612, rumours began circulating to the effect that he had been murdered, rumours which were stronger and seemingly more plausible than

Passion, Poison and Power

the doubts which commonly arose in those days upon the death of one so young and healthy. Weldon, for example, referred to 'that most hopeful Prince Henry, who dyed not without vehement suspicion of Poyson'. Even the late Prince's chaplain hinted at his violent death. Coke's publicly expressed suspicions on the point caused Weldon to wonder whether the judge might have 'lighted on some papers, that spake plain in that which was ever whispered'. Something which gave legs to the murder theory was the fact that a potion called Raleigh's 'elixir of life' (possibly quinine) had been given to the Prince *in extremis*: it was 'known' to cure any fever *except poison,* and it had failed in the case of the Prince; *ergo*, concluded popular opinion, he must have been poisoned. But who would have had reason for killing this popular young man?

The historian, Thomas Birch, reported a contemporary who pointed the finger of suspicion at unnamed persons 'who perhaps ... fearing the growing virtues of that young Prince, have used the traitorous venom of their abominable practices to cut him off in his youth'. Anne Turner was more specific when she told the investigators that the Prince had been poisoned with a bunch of grapes administered by a physician with a red beard. (Franklin, who sometimes claimed to be a pharmacist, had a red beard.)[9]

Some suspected Carr of having had a hand in the Prince's death. According to Rimbault, 'A great enmity certainly subsisted between Somerset and the Prince, whatever were the grounds of it'. The ever-dramatic Wilson asserted that 'some that knew the hickerings between the Prince and the Viscount [Carr] muttered out dark sentences that durst not look into the light; especially,

---

[9] Even Mayerne seems to have been disturbed. Everything that related to Prince Henry's last illness was torn out of his collection of cases (Andrew Amos, *The Great Oyer of Poisoning: The Trial of the Earl of Somerset for the possible poisoning of Sir Thomas Overbury* (London, Richard Bentley, 1846)).

The Conspiracy Theories

Sir James Elphington, who (observing the Prince one day to be discontented with the Viscount) offered to kill him: but the Prince reproved him with a gallant spirit, saying, "If there were cause he would do it himself.""'.[10] Henry certainly had grounds for disliking Carr, notably his unwelcome support for the Prince's marriage to a Spanish princess, Salisbury's hints that he was frustrating the Prince's ambitions in Council, and, of course, his success in engaging the attentions of Frances Essex. Even when added together, however, they hardly amount to grounds for murder.

Others favoured Overbury as the culprit. A contemporary wrote that Henry 'does utterly dislike him, forbears his company, and ... falls flat at odds with him, not once giving him any countenance of vouchsafing him his company'.[11] According to Sir Simonds D'Ewes, there was 'a constant report' among the Scots that:

> 'Overbury, seeing divers crossings and oppositions to happen between that peerless Prince and the said Rochester, by whose means only he expected to rise; and fearing it would in the end be a means to ruin Rochester himself, did first give that damnable and fatal advice of removing out of the way and world that royal youth by fascination, and was himself afterwards in part an instrument for the effecting of it ...'[12]

Those prone to putting two and two together to make five were not slow to conclude that Overbury had been killed by the King in revenge for the murder of his son, the Prince. It was even rumoured that the King had had his own son killed. This seems to have been based on no more than James' reference to the Prince

---

[10] Arthur Wilson, *History of Great Britain, Being the Life and Reign of King James I* (Richard Lownds, 1653).
[11] Michael Sparke, *The Narrative History of King James for the First Fourteen Years* (London, Michael Sparke, 1651).
[12] Sir Simonds D'Ewes, *The Autobiography and Correspondence of Sir Simonds D'Ewes Bt.,* James Orchard Halliwell (ed.) (London, Richard Bentley, 1845).

Passion, Poison and Power

(quoted by Roger Coke), 'What? Will he bury me alive?' And the facts, according to Amos, that the King never visited Henry during his last sickness, and after his death banned mourning at court. But these are ridiculous foundations for such an improbable notion.

Fortunately, the condition of the Prince's body is well documented in the report of Mayerne and the other doctors who conducted the post-mortem examination. They found:

1. That his liver was more pale than it should be, and in divers places wan, and like lead; and the gall-bladder was without gall and choler, and full of wind.
2. His spleen was in divers places unnaturally black.
3. His stomach was without any manner of fault or imperfection.
4. His midriff was in many places blackish.
5. His lungs were black, and in many places spotted, and full of much corruption.
6. He had the veins of the hinder part of his head too full of blood, and the passages and hollow places of his brain full of much clear water.[13]

These findings, coupled with the symptoms which the Prince displayed immediately prior to his death, all point to his having suffered from typhoid fever. (The spleen is one of the organs where the typhoid bacterium, a species of salmonella, reproduces.) The infection was most probably contracted after swimming in the river Thames, which in those days was little more than an open sewer.

So much for conspiracy theory.[14]

---

[13] Thomas Birch, *The Life of Henry, Prince of Wales* (London, A. Miller, 1760).
[14] Conspiracy theorists do not seem to realize that the more theories that are put forward the less convincing becomes the case for any one.

ACT 13

WHO OR WHAT KILLED OVERBURY?

So what, after all these investigations, trials and memoirs, do we really know about how and why Sir Thomas Overbury met his unpleasant death? In one sense very little, since almost everyone concerned, even the innocent, played their hands close to their chests, making every effort to conceal their true feelings, their hidden desires. Nevertheless, James and his advisers were confident that they knew the truth of it all: at the behest of Northampton, Carr and Frances had plotted to have Overbury locked up and pressured to agree to the annulment. When it became clear that he would never submit they decided to resort to the ultimate sanction and hired staff for the task. Various powders and 'waters' having failed to do the job, they finished off their victim with a poisoned enema.

This scenario, which was the one put forward at Carr's trial, has too many holes to be convincing. It does not explain why the murderers should have gone to the lengths of an elaborate plot to get their intended victim into the Tower when they could as easily have killed him outside. It does not explain why, if they were going to kill him they should spend so much time trying to change his mind over the annulment. It does not explain why the poisoning attempts began before it became apparent that Overbury would never bend to their will. It does not explain why Overbury fell ill in the Tower long before it was clear that he would not change his mind. Nor does it explain how Frances' plans fitted into that of Northampton and her husband. Let us begin by considering what is certain, or as near certain as our limited knowledge allows.

One thing we can be sure of is that Frances desperately wished to see Overbury dead and did what she could to poison him, not once but repeatedly and in an imaginative variety of ways. As the daughter of one of England's most noble families, she was affronted at being frustrated by the puffed-up, unlikeable son of a commoner. As one of the most admired women at court, she was deeply hurt by his abuse of her character. As someone desperate to remarry, she was only too aware of his potential to destroy her hopes of an annulment, or to ruin her afterwards should it be granted.

We have already dismissed the idea that it was Carr who had Overbury murdered: that leaves Northampton. Admittedly his great niece wanted the knight dead, but It is impossible to imagine a powerful man like the Earl agreeing to murder simply in order to satisfy the passions of a young woman. What then was his motivation? Northampton had his own grievance against Overbury. Until Carr arrived on the scene he had occupied a position of power and influence unrivalled in the land, a position which Carr threatened by his proximity to the King and by his known Catholic leaning tendencies. Northampton decided to deal with the threat by marrying his great niece off to the King's new Favourite, who was already smitten with her, but before that could happen it was necessary to release Frances from her first marriage. Overbury's publicly declared opposition to the annulment and his persistent defaming of Frances' character made him a real obstacle to this plan so Northampton decided to get him out of the way, first by removing him from the country, but when that failed by having him incarcerated as someone who had defied his monarch. It was a course of action which Carr seems to have been only too willing to fall in with.

It is easy to see what this must have looked like from the prosecution's point of view. Coke's interrogations had brought to light Carr's involvement in the plot to imprison Overbury and his desperate attempts to destroy or mutilate evidence, as well as Frances' vindictive attempts to poison the prisoner. The obvious conclusion was that her husband was also party to the poison plot. It was a scenario which involved many inconsistencies and improbabilities, but from the moment that Frances confessed her guilt the prosecution were relieved of the task of explaining them.

AN ALTERNATIVE HYPOTHESIS

But what if Bacon had been mistaken in lumping Frances' conspiracy to murder in with the conspiracy to imprison and 'turn' Overbury? What if there was, not one, but two entirely different conspiracies directed against Overbury at the same time, the members of each were unaware of the others' intentions?

In this scenario, Overbury was thrown into the Tower at the instigation of Northampton and Carr for the purpose of pressuring him into assenting to the annulment of Frances' marriage. While the two men were aware of Frances' spiteful fury towards their victim, there is no evidence that they were aware it was strong enough to lead her to try to kill him. Frances must have been overjoyed when she learned that Overbury had been delivered into her hands bound and gagged, so to speak. Not only was he close confined, but his gaoler was a former employee of Frances' companion, Anne Turner, who had also been the go-between in the early days of her affair with Carr. This may have been just good fortune – from Frances' point of view – or it may have been because she had suggested Weston's name to her husband as an amenable tool; we can only speculate. Whichever was the case, with Weston in place and with the willing assistance of Anne, Frances was in a position to wreak revenge on her tormentor, at the same time getting rid of the only obstacle in the way of her annulment. (The Ecclesiastical Commission met for the first time barely three weeks after Overbury entered the Tower.)

For their part, Carr and Northampton would not have thought it necessary, or even desirable, to involve Frances in their plans for Overbury, although it is possible that she got to know of them from her lover's pillow talk. It was not in Frances' nature to divulge her plans to others. (Remember that she had had two men secretly dosed with magic potions with a view to stimulating or abating their lust for her.) While she may or may not have been aware of what her husband and her great uncle were up to together, they appear to have acted in complete ignorance of her murderous intentions toward their prisoner.

Months later, just as Overbury seemed to be on the point of agreeing to the annulment, he made it clear that his cooperation was neither willing nor reliable. At this point his health, which had been in decline for some time, took a turn for the worse. (We will consider why later.) Northampton could not conceal his delight, but Carr appears to have been genuinely concerned at the suffering of his old friend and took steps to help him with food and medical attention. When the unfortunate man died both conspirators must have been terrified that the finger of suspicion would point at them, not for what they had done – an elaborate plot to facilitate the annulment – but for what they would appear to have done, murder most foul. Northampton ran around getting rid of the incriminating cadaver. Much later when Carr came under suspicion he did all he could to destroy or doctor any scraps of evidence that might incriminate him.

The idea of two parallel plots explains many puzzling aspects of the Overbury story, in particular Elwes' strange conduct when he came across Weston bearing the poisoned glass. Though privy to his masters' plot to 'turn' Overbury, he must have been fearful that he might by accident have stumbled on a far more sinister objective of theirs from which he had been deliberately excluded; and so, instead of reporting what he had found, he contented himself with berating the intended poisoner and with frustrating his plans by substituting edible for poisoned food. It is only the separate nature of the two plots that permits us to understand the full significance of Carr's description of the Lieutenant as 'the worst deserver in this business; an unoffended instrument might have prevented all after-mischief, who for his own ends suffered it, and by the like arts afterward betrayed it'. If only he had spoken to Carr after coming across Weston with the poisoned 'water' the Earl could have put a stop to his wife's murderous plans, Overbury might not have died in agony, the 'little fishes' would not have been hanged and the Somersets would have been saved from imprisonment and disgrace.

But it was not to be. Frances was allowed to carry on with her attempts to poison and when the prisoner died his body displayed all the symptoms of poisoning. It may seem curious therefore that we still have to ask, who or what caused the death of Overbury?

HOW DID OVERBURY DIE?

There was a rumour put about at the time of Overbury's death that he had died of venereal disease and that his body was found to be 'leprosed with vice'. Both assertions are inconsistent with the dead man's medical history and with the state of his corpse and may have been lies designed to blacken his character and possibly even throw people off the trail. There are contemporary reports which point to Overbury having suffered from consumption, or as we now know it, tuberculosis. This was the diagnosis of a doctor on 14 June 1613, some three months before his death, and Dr Anthony expressed a similar view later that month. Loubell's father repeated the claim, presumably having heard it from his son. However, if Overbury's lungs were, indeed, tubercular there was little from a medical point of view to suggest that it was this which killed him.[1]

But could ill health in any way have contributed to his death?

Overbury seems to have taken a gloomy view of his own constitution. '[W]hiles I was abroad', he wrote, '[I] was never well, ... as Mayerus knows, which made me returne so soone ...'. A more balanced view was given by two of his long-term servants, Davies and Payton, who told the investigators that prior to his imprisonment their master 'was very healthful, and never kept his bed for any sickness, only he was sometimes troubled with the spleen, for ease whereof, he had by the advice of his physician an issue made in his left arm; but before his imprisonment, he had no sores, blisters, or other defects in all his body'.[2] (Keeping a vein open for bleeding was then regarded as a treatment of the spleen.) We should also remember that health problems, particularly concerning his spleen, were one of the reasons which Overbury advanced for refusing the embassy post. We can discount the prisoner's claim to Carr that he was 'possessed of a dangerous disease'. Weston claimed that when he was admitted to the Tower, Overbury had 'a most disabled and unhealthful body', but the evidence of a hired murderer has to be taken with a pinch of salt, particularly when it is flatly contradicted by other sources. On 3 July 1613, while making a bath 'to cool his body' Loubell noted that the prisoner's skin was 'very exceeding fair and clear'.

---

[1] There is an unpleasant form of tuberculosis known as miliary tuberculosis which can give rise to diarrhoea and, if associated with fever, vomiting also, but this is mercifully rare. (Today, this accounts for possibly some 1% to 3% of all cases.)

[2] Under the mediaeval theory of the four humours, over-activity of the spleen led to what was called black bile which was believed to be the cause of melancholy.

After death the prisoner's body was in a quite different state. Loubell found it to be 'full of blisters, and so consumed away, as he never saw the like'. Elwes provided an even more detailed picture, 'Overbury being viewed, there was found in his arm an issue, and on his belly twelve kernels likely to break to issue, each as big as a three-pence; one issue on his back, with a tawny plaister on it; this was strange and ugly. He stunk intolerably, in so much that he was cast into the coffin with a loose sheet over him'. This account was confirmed by a jury of twelve, six of them warders,[3] convened by Robert Bright, the coroner, to conduct an inquest the morning Overbury died. They found the cadaver to be 'so bare that in effect it was consumed away, having nothing but skin and bones, and the body very lank. There was a black ulcer the width of two fingers between the shoulder blades, an issue kept open by a little bullet of gold on the left arm and a plaster on the sole of his feet. And on his belly were yellow blisters as big as peas'. What caused the body to be in such a parlous state?

Anne Somerset considered – only to dismiss – a number of other conditions that might have killed the prisoner, including septicaemia secondary to a gangrenous ulcer, and late onset diabetes. The symptoms of his suffering and the state of his body *post mortem* all seem to point in one direction only, death by poisoning.

DEATH BY POISONING?

Poison had been in use in the courts of Europe since at least the days of the Borgias as a means of getting rid of personal and political enemies. Because it did not require physical violence, it was the instrument of choice for women. We know that Frances pas-

---

[3] Sir Simonds D'Ewes reports that the others were prisoners.

Passion, Poison and Power

sionately' wanted Overbury dead and did all she could to poison him. It is no wonder therefore that the prosecution concluded that he died as a result. But was this in fact the case?

Until the nineteenth century the only method of detecting the presence of poison in a dead body was to administer a sample of whatever remained of the suspect substance to a dog or cat and observe the effects. No such test was undertaken with Overbury. Our only hope of identifying the cause of death, therefore, is to consider what substances were administered to the prisoner, beginning with the poisons which Frances is known to have employed.

In his opening speech at Carr's trial, Bacon had accused the Earl of administering rosalgar in 'a kind of broth', white arsenic in food, and mercury sublimate mixed into tarts and jellies, as well as in the form of a clyster. According to the notes for the speech which the ever-thorough Attorney prepared for Frances' trial but never delivered, 'white arsenic was fit for salt, because it is of like body and colour. The poison of great spiders, and of the venomous fly cantharides, was fit for pigs sauce, or partridge sauce, because it resembled pepper. As for mercury-water and other poisons, they might be fit for tarts, which is a kind of hotch-pot, wherein no one colour is so proper'.

There is no doubt that the poisons were intended for Overbury's consumption, but, we must ask, how many of them did the intended victim actually ingest? Observing that some of the tarts, after standing awhile, turned 'black and foul' Elwes drew the obvious conclusion that they had been poisoned and had them 'counterfeited, and others sent to be presented in their stead ...'. Weston bore him out in this by asserting that the tarts 'which came from the Countess were thrown away by him and the Lieutenant, supposing them naught in regard of the colour, and that the Countess forbade him [that is, Weston] to touch them; that those which came from [Carr] were good and of every one he

[Weston] did eat his part'. How Overbury died, Weston concluded, 'God knew, he knew not'.[4] If he was telling the truth, and there is no reason to doubt him on this, the remarkable implication would seem to be that Overbury may never have eaten or drunk any significant quantity of the poisons which had been sent to him by Frances, a conclusion which, of course, accords well with the fact that the prisoner, though ill, remained obstinately alive.

According to the prosecution, Frances' final and fatal attempt at murder was by mercury for a second time, but introduced into the body in an altogether different manner.

THE TALE OF THE POISONED ENEMA

Possibly the most dramatic feature surrounding Overbury's fate is the tale of the poisoned clyster, but the actual facts, like so much in this story, are difficult to pin down. According to the prosecution, the fourth and final attempt on the prisoner's life was made in mid-September 1613. Elwes arranged on the thirteenth of the month to have the prisoner's clothes sent to his cell so that they would, in accordance with the custom of the day, become his upon the prisoner's death. (It was one of the most incriminating pieces of evidence against the Lieutenant.) The following day Weston and an unidentified apothecary were said to have administered mercury sublimate 'into the guts of the said Sir T'. By the following day he was dead.

The official version of events set out in Weston's indictment was more detailed:

---

[4] John Holles to the Duke of Lennox, 20 December 1615, in John Holles, *Letters of John Holles,* P.R. Seddon (ed.) (Nottingham, Derry and Sons, 1975).

'Weston and another man, being an apothecary, ... upon the 14th of September, feloniously did get a poison called Mercury Sublimate (knowing the same to be deadly poison) and put the same into a clyster mingled with the same poison; and the said clyster the said apothecary, for the reward of £20 promised unto him did put and minister (as good and wholesome) into the guts of said sir T. and that Weston was present and aiding to the said apothecary in ministering and infusing the said clyster; and that immediately after, as well the taking of the said poisoned meats, and ministering the said clyster the said sir T did languish and fell into diseases and distempers; and from the aforesaid times of taking and eating the said poisoned meats, and ministering the said clyster, he died.'

The words 'mingled with the same poison' suggest that the mercury sent as poison had been added to a mercury clyster which, presumably, was being administered for normal medical reasons. Now this clyster cannot be the same one which Weston told the investigators had been given to the prisoner by Loubell only 'two or three days' before his death. Almost all we know about the last, or 'fatal', enema is contained in Weston's admission to Elwes, as confirmed in outline by the mendacious Franklin. But before this story can be accepted it has to overcome a major difficulty. A contemporary writing after the trial recorded that Weston had denied in court that Overbury had in fact been given the enema as Franklin claimed, or that 'any potticarie [had] meddled with Overbury save the potticarie appointed by Mr Mairne'.[5] Nothing like this appears in *The State Trials,* yet it is consistent with the Lieutenant's instructions, as reported by Weston, that no one except Loubell or his assistant should attend Overbury or administer any clyster.

It seems that the whole poisoned enema story may be as apocryphal as the red hot poker which was supposed to have been introduced into Edward II at the same point of entry. But if

---

[5] Letter of 20 December 1615, in *Letters of John Holles, ibid.*

Overbury was not killed by tainted food or a deliberately poisoned enema, how did he die?

AN ALTERNATIVE HYPOTHESIS

A mercury clyster was one of the favourite remedies of seventeenth-century physicians. It was considered to be particularly efficacious for syphilis, on the analogy of its supposed effectiveness in treating scabies and other skin diseases. More significantly, it was also used for the relief of constipation, which is a condition common among people living in confinement, as noted in Overbury's 'character' essay, *A Prisoner*:

> 'Whatsoever his complexion was before, it turnes (in this place) to choler or deepe melancholy, so that hee needs every houre to take physick to loose his body, for that (like his estate) is very foule and corrupt, and extremely hard bound. The taking of an execution off his stomack, gives him five or six stooles, and leaves his body very soluble.'

It is unlikely that Overbury himself wrote that essay for the reasons noted above. In any event it would appear to be an accurate observation of the health of prisoners in general.

As long ago as 1600, Mayerne had written a thesis espousing 'the use of mineral medicines, particularly the antinomials and mercurials' for this problem.[6] We do not know in what strength Mayerne prescribed this enema, but he famously favoured his remedies strong. Overbury is known to have received a number of them while in the Tower, probably for constipation. But the full dangers of mercury were not known at that time and we cannot ignore the possibility that it was over-enthusiasm in the use of

---

[6] 'Antinomials' and 'mercurials' were remedies based respectively on antimony and mercury.

mercury enemas that killed him, or at least contributed to his death, particularly if he had been receiving mercury from another source.

And he had.

'DRINKABLE GOLD'

While in the Tower Overbury is known to have taken, on a number of occasions and in addition to the mercury enemas, a popular 'remedy' of the time known as aurum potabile, or 'drinkable gold'. Aurum potabile was a nostrum dreamed up by the renowned Hermetic practitioner, Paracelsus, and in Overbury's day was the cure-all remedy of a quack physician by the name of Francis Anthony (1550–1623).

Anthony was the son of a goldsmith who practised out of St Bartholomew's the Great and other places. He was often in trouble with the College of Physicians and was imprisoned more than once for practising medicine without a licence. It did not stop him and in 1602 the College recorded him as having 'Confessed to practice [sic] for 3 years in London. Had lately treated Ward and Roger Cotton's servant, leaving one dead and the other dangerously ill'. In 1606, Anthony was found guilty of giving a priest 'a chemical medicament' causing 'vomiting, diarrhoea and death'. In 1609, the President of the College announced that 'many complaints' had been received against him. (He escaped some of them by the simple expedient of not turning up at the disciplinary hearing!) Aurum potabile had featured in a number of the allegations and in 1609 the College commissioned Sir Thomas Knyvett, warden of the king's mint, to hold a trial of its efficacy, though it produced no conclusive result.[7] Eventually, Anthony obtained the qualification

---

[7] F.V. White in *Oxford Dictionary of National Biography* (Oxford, Oxford University Press, 2004) hints that Knyvett may not have been impartial.

of MD and was able to practise medicine without interference from the College of Physicians. He swiftly became rich with the help of royal patronage.

As with many alchemical substances, aurum potabile was made by an immensely complex process, but in essence it was simply powdered gold and mercury mixed (or, as the practitioners would have it, dissolved) in wine or vinegar. According to Anthony, it was a sovereign remedy against most human ills, ranging from sterility, plague, dropsy, jaundice and the palsy, down to insomnia, besides being a prophylactic. Its inefficacy as a medicine was finally exposed in 1623 by the Northampton physician, John Cotta, in his book, *Cotta Contra Antonium*, in which he analysed and destroyed Anthony's claims for the nostrum, listing the names of various people who had been killed by it.[8] Overbury is known to have been among Anthony's clients while he was in the Tower.

According to Anthony when questioned by the Commissioners, one of Sir Thomas' servants had come to him wanting to know whether aurum potabile 'was good against poison?'. Assured that it was, the servant had bought two ounces of it for £10, later reporting that 'it had done his master good'. Despite Carr's assertion to the contrary, Overbury also seems to have obtained the substance from the Earl, since on 26 July 1613 Lidcote reported to him that 'Overbury hath taken all of your Lordship's aurum potabile ... and surely finds much good of it'.[9]

---

[8] John Cotta, *Cotta contra Antonium: or an Ant-Antony: or an Ant-apology, manifesting Doctor Antony his Apologie for Aurum potable, in true and equal balance of right reason, to be false and counterfait* (Oxford, J. Lichfield & J. Sort for H. Cripps, 1623). The book was a refutation of Francis Anthony, *The Apologie, or, defence of a verity heretofore published concerning a medicine called Aurum Potabile* (London, J. Legatt,1616).
[9] Sir John Lidcote to Viscount Rochester. Samuel R. Gardiner, *History of England from the Accession of James I to the Outbreak of the Civil War, 1603–1642*, Vol. 2 (London, Longman, Green and Co, 1883).

Passion, Poison and Power

Could self-medication with aurum potabile have been the inadvertent cause of Overbury's death, or at least a contributory factor? The gold and the vinegar were unlikely to have done him much harm, but the mercury could have had serious consequences, depending on quantity and on whatever amounts of the metal he was ingesting from other sources. What then are the effects of mercury on the human body?

Mercuric chloride or corrosive sublimate, can take the form of a white powder, granules or a colourless crystal. It has a pronounced acrid taste which would be readily detectable by anyone eating it. Taken orally, it can induce vomiting and abdominal pain. Large doses can cause blisters in the mouth and throat, bloody diarrhoea and internal haemorrhaging, leading to circulatory failure, respiratory distress and acute renal failure. A nineteenth-century medical authority who examined the role of mercury in the Overbury case, concluded: 'We have reason to believe, from the result of experiments on animals, that the effects of the poison administered [anally] would be similar to [oral ingestion]'.[10]

It seems likely from the dead man's symptoms and from the condition of his body after death that Overbury suffered from mercury poisoning to such an extent that it could have been fatal, but was it mercury that finally killed him? There is some evidence that, whatever poisons Overbury had consumed, the proximate cause of death might have been something entirely different.

WAS OVERBURY SMOTHERED?

Some contemporary sources suggest that, whether he was poisoned or not, Overbury may actually have died from an altogether

---

[10] Theodric Romeyn Beck, *Elements of Medical Jurisprudence*, 2nd edn, William Dunlop (ed.) (London, John Anderson, 1825).

different cause. Anne Turner may have been referring to this when she told the minister who attended her after conviction that Weston, when asked if Overbury was dead, had replied, 'No. Not yet, but I will now go and send the knave away packing. I will pull away his pillow and then be gone'. Sir Simonds D'Ewes had heard something similar, though he was inclined to dismiss it as unsupported by sworn testimony. Weldon came up with an altogether more detailed narrative:

> '[Weston and Franklin] came into Overburies Chamber, and found him in infinite torment, with contention between the strength of Nature, and the working of the Poyson, and it being very like, Nature had gotten the better in that contention, by the thrusting out of boyls, botches, and blains [an inflamed swelling on the skin], they fearing it might come to light, upon the judgement of Phisitians, that foul play had been offered him, consented to stifle him with the Bed-cloaths, which accordingly was performed, and so ended his miserable life, with the assurance of the Conspirators, that he dyed by poison; none thinking otherwise, but these two Murtherers.'[11]

While the story may be no more than rumour, we cannot dismiss entirely the idea that those who were employed to poison Overbury ended his life prematurely in a way which no one at the time suspected out of fear that, if his sufferings were allowed to continue, their involvement in his poisoning would have been exposed.

If Overbury died from accidental mercury poisoning as a result of mercury clysters aggravated by his consumption of aurum potabile, or even as a result of smothering, the extraordinary implication is that the Somersets, husband and wife, were wrongly convicted and that their accomplices were wrongly executed, whether they believed this to be the case or not.

---

[11] Weldon, Sir Anthony *The Court and Character of King James I*, 1650 reprinted in *The Secret History of the Court of James I* (Sir Walter Scott, ed).

ACT 14

AND AFTERWARDS?

Coke's standing at court never recovered from his impolitic conduct of Monson's trial. After the Somersets had been convicted, charges were brought against him which resulted in his dismissal from the Bench. Although his place remains secure as one of the pillars of the common law, Coke must have died in 1634 with the taste of failure in his mouth. His rival Bacon's fall from grace was even more humiliating. After becoming Lord Chancellor and having been raised to the peerage, his career ended in disgrace when in 1620 he confessed to having taken bribes. Despite his excuse that he had been 'frail, and partak[ing] of the abuse of the times', he was fined heavily, briefly imprisoned and barred for life from any public office. So ended the career of the man whom Alexander Pope judged 'The wisest, brightest, meanest of mankind'.[12]

Suffolk proved to be an embarrassment to Buckingham, and in 1619 he and his avaricious wife were convicted of corruption, imprisoned for a short period and fined heavily. This particular generation of Howards were never to embarrass their monarch again.

---

[12] Alexander Pope, *Essay on Man*, Epistle 4.

And Afterwards?

The enigmatic Sir Thomas Monson was allowed to kiss hands in 1620, but he never regained his former status at court and financial troubles kept him in relative penury up to the time of his death in 1641.

Essex re-married in 1630, but the couple soon separated following stories of his wife's adultery. His day of glory was yet to come: during England's terrible civil war he became Captain General of the Parliamentary army in its struggle against King Charles, the son of James, but resigned his post in 1645 following disagreements with Cromwell. He died of a stroke the following year.

After a long and debilitating illness, Queen Anne died in 1619, largely estranged from her husband who continued to be infatuated with what proved to be his last lover, Buckingham. James himself lived on, suffering from increasingly painful kidney problems and arthritis. Following a stroke, he died of dysentery on 27 March 1625. Three years later Buckingham, who, it was said, 'since his first being a pretty, harmless, affable gentleman', had grown 'insolent, cruel, and a monster not to be endured',[1] was assassinated by a mentally disturbed officer.

As already noted, Frances died in 1632 at the age of thirty nine. Her husband Robert survived her by thirteen years, having witnessed, no doubt bitterly, the unrelenting rise of Villiers. Their daughter, Anne, was brought up in ignorance of her parents' disgrace and is said to have fainted when she learned of it from a book. She nevertheless went on to become one of the great beauties of King Charles's court, marrying the Duke of Bedford in 1637.

Thomas Overbury's father, Nicholas, died in 1643 at about the age of one hundred.

---

[1] Weldon, Sir Anthony *The Court and Character of King James I*, 1650 reprinted in *The Secret History of the Court of James I* (Sir Walter Scott, ed).

Passion, Poison and Power

Having served as medical adviser to four Kings, Dr Mayerne took his secrets to the grave at the age of eighty-two.

ENVOI

And so, one by one, our cast has left the stage. No one shed a tear for the villain, Weston or the fantasist, Franklin. Anne Turner commanded the sympathy of the groundlings only by the brave way in which she met her death. The former Lieutenant of the Tower, the ingenuous Gervase Elwes, died believing that 'by divers tricks [he had been] drawn into this action'. Tricked he may have been, but his betrayal of his office and his willingness to bully his prisoner into submission while turning a blind eye to what he knew or believed were attempts to kill him must remove any inclination we might have to pity. Thomas Monson mysteriously escaped justice by the skin of his teeth, while Northampton, who was at the heart of the plot to imprison Overbury, was saved from disgrace by simple mortality. But what of the two leading actors?

Frances was widely portrayed in her time as a stereotypical female monster, consumed by lust, whose death was God's punishment for a lascivious life. Sparke, for example, called her 'a woman ... of a lustful appetite, prodigal of expence, covetous of applause, ambitious of honor, and light of behaviour'. Carr, by contrast, was let off lightly as 'subjecting himself to the lustful appetite of an evill woman'. Modern day opinion is more forgiving. We cannot be certain, for example, exactly what pressures Frances was put under by her great uncle for his own ends. A bright, pretty little flower, she was trapped from an early age in a loveless marriage not of her choosing and no one can criticize her for wanting to be out of it. Nevertheless, she forfeits our sympathy for believing that her desires justified murdering the man who stood in her way.

And Afterwards?

Contrary to the finding of the court, there is no reason to disbelieve Robert Carr's protestations that he had no part in Overbury's death and participated in the plot to imprison him only in order to prevent him hindering Frances' intended annulment. He seems to have done what he could to make his friend's incarceration tolerable and when the latter became ill, was at pains to see that he received proper medical attention. He supported Overbury's attempt to gain the King's mercy by trickery, even to the extent of taking the vomit inducing powder himself. As the prisoner's health started to fail he must have begun to suspect that other more sinister forces were at play. Carr was understandably terrified to learn of his death, believing all too correctly that he would fall under suspicion, not merely for the betrayal, but for the murder of a friend. It is little wonder that he tried all the tricks in the book to avoid being put on trial, and the ensuing conviction must have been an intolerable burden for him, mitigated only somewhat by his subsequent pardon and partial rehabilitation.

Carr had little to recommend himself except a fine figure and the love of his Sovereign. When this ended, as such things do, he felt betrayed but, instead of gracefully departing the scene ,for which he would have been well rewarded by the ever-generous James, he chose the path of jealousy and pique, going out of his way to berate, even threaten, the source of his honours and wealth. He was in other words truly the author of his own misfortune. Carr can justifiably be accused of pride, selfishness, mendacity and disloyalty, but it seems unlikely that he was a murderer or even plotted murder.

James was the most complex character of them all. The victim of a damaged childhood with at the very least homosexual tendencies, he chose to sublimate his sexuality by condemning the 'sin' of homosexuality. Perhaps it would have been expecting too much of anyone with his background and in his day to have done otherwise. A more than usually intelligent and sensitive man, he nevertheless allowed himself to be swayed by the self-serving flattery of his courtiers. He seems to have been genuinely astonished and hurt when he learned that his former Favourite was suspected of murder of the worst kind. Convinced that the Earl and his wife were guilty of a foul crime, he was determined to ensure their convictions, but equally determined that, once convicted, they should, if consistent with honour, be saved from the penalty prescribed by law. The subsequent pardoning of the principal offenders after the execution of those they had used as their tools seems to modern eyes to be an act of egregious injustice, but it was hardly exceptional in an age when 'nobility' was a question of genealogy rather than spirit. James' final resting place was lost until his body was discovered many years later bundled into the tomb of Henry VII in Westminster Abbey. A tablet describes him fittingly in Latin as 'The enigma of the world'. Nearby stands the gilded effigy of Villiers lying beside that of his lawful wife,[2] almost opposite that of James' other lover, Esmé Stewart, First Duke of Lennox and his wife.

Even now, we cannot be sure of the cause of Overbury's death. While a number of determined attempts were made to poison him, there is no proof that any of them brought about his death and much that they did not. A more likely cause was iatrogenic poisoning from the mercury in the enemas which had been innocently administered for his constipation, aggravated by consumption of Doctor Anthony's lethal brew. He may even have been smothered at the last by villains anxious to conceal what they believed to be the consequences of their crimes.

Overbury was a capable man with a keen but cruel wit and, which often goes with it, a ready ability to make enemies. In Oldisworth's words, 'He expected more of life than life had to give, and thus was constantly out of humour with his surroundings. He contemned always that which was nearest to him, and detected with the quick eye of criticism the weakness and folly of his intimate companions'. He was ill advised in going out of his way to offend at the same time both those who could ruin him and those who could save him. In his short life Overbury made many enemies, but it seems unlikely that he died at the hands of those

---

[2] His heart and brain were buried in Portsmouth cathedral.

convicted of his murder. It is little consolation for such a lonely and miserable death.

AUTHOR'S NOTE

Who or what killed Overbury are questions that have fascinated people for centuries. Answering them is made more difficult, not merely by the temporal gap between us and the Jacobean age, but by the vastly different moral values of the times, the scarcity of definitive evidence and the lies and obfuscations of so many concerned. Why then do we need another book on this subject, and from a lawyer, not a historian?

Central to our knowledge of Overbury's story are the trials that followed his death. As a lawyer, I hope I have been able to bring a particular understanding to the attitudes and motivations of the early practitioners of my craft, the fundamentals of which have not changed as much as some might imagine over the past five hundred years.

I have sought to employ a forensic approach in judging where the truth lies, preferring the earlier to the later account, the evidence of the disinterested to that of the *partis pris* and that of the honest man to that of the proven liar. I have followed Cicero in trying to work out who stands to gain from any action. And I have not been slow to wield Occam's razor, favouring the simpler over the more complex explanation of events. While accepting completely Anne Somerset's observation that, 'It is, quite simply, impossible to ascertain the full truth of the case of Sir Thomas Overbury', I

Author's Note

venture to suggest that the solution I have arrived at fits the facts more closely than any of the others so far proposed.[1]

I cannot claim to have unearthed dramatic new sources (indeed, it seems unlikely that there are any remaining to be found), but I have always sought to use the most nearly contemporaneous records available. I have made only minimal changes to seventeenth-century spelling and phraseology; to my mind they add colour to the picture of their time. Central to my interpretation of the mystery has been the role of the notorious Dr Anthony, which has not always received the attention it deserves. The archives of the College of Surgeons have been particularly enlightening in this connection.

I should explain why I have adopted the conceit of presenting this book in the style of a Jacobean drama. Overbury's brief, but extraordinary story was punctuated throughout by 'masques' (which are a form of play), followed by courtroom scenes (which bear comparison with theatrical performances) and the gallows (which is merely a stage surrounded by an enthusiastic audience). The most famous court scandal in the reign of James I – and many others if truth be told – can, I suggest, truly be described as a Jacobean tragedy.

I trust that even those who do not share my view of how poor Overbury died will take pleasure in reading this account of his extraordinary life and horrible death.

Brian Harris QC

---

[1] For a concise list of alternative readings see John Emsley, *The Elements of Murder: A History of Poison* (Oxford, Oxford University Press, 2005), pp. 88 and 89.

PRINCIPAL SOURCES

Amos, Andrew, *The Great Oyer of Poisoning: The Trial of the Earl of Somerset for the possible poisoning of Sir Thomas Overbury* (London, Richard Bentley, 1846). Amos held the chair of English law at University College, London from 1827 to 1834, becoming Downing Professor of the Laws of England in 1849. 'The great oyer of poisoning' as a description of the Overbury trials was a term coined by Sir Edward Coke.

Bellany, Alastair, *The Politics of Court in Early Modern England: News Culture and the Overbury Affair, 1603–1660* (Cambridge, Cambridge University Press, 2002).

Cook, Judith, *Dr Simon Forman; a most notorious physician* (London, Vintage, 2002).

Devereux, Walter Bourchier, *Lives and Letters of the Devereux, Earls of Essex. In the Reigns of Elizabeth, James I, and Charles I, 1540–1646*, Vol. 2 (London, Adamant Media Corporation, 2005).

D'Ewes, Sir Simonds, *The Autobiography and Correspondence of Sir Simonds D'Ewes Bt.,* James Orchard Halliwell (ed.) (London, Richard Bentley, 1845). D'Ewes was an antiquarian, diarist and Member of Parliament for the Puritan faction. We should remember that at the time of Overbury's death he would have been only eleven years old. Nevertheless, he appears to have been a level-headed recorder of events.

Principal Sources

Ellis, George E., *Bacon's Dictionary of Boston with an Historical Introduction* (Boston and New York, Houghton Mifflin and Co., 1886).

The Harleian Miscellany (London, 1810). This important collection is subtitled, *'A Collection of Scarce, Curious, And Entertaining Pamphlets And Tracts, as well In Manuscript As In Print, Found In The Late Earl Of Oxford's Library, Interspersed With Historical, Political, And Critical Notes.* The Harley library was founded in October 1704, when Robert Harley purchased more than 600 manuscripts from the collection of Sir Simonds d'Ewes.

Holles, John, *Letters of John Holles,* P.R. Seddon (ed.) (Nottingham, Derry and Sons, 1975).

Lindley, David, *The Trials of Frances Howard: Fact and Fiction at the Court of King James* (New York, Routledge, 1993).

Matter, Joseph Allen, *My Lords and Lady of Essex: Their State Trials* (Chicago, Henry Regnery Company, 1969).

Oldisworth, Nicholas, *A booke touching Sir Thomas Overbury* (1637). A note in the British Museum manuscript of this work declares that 'I Nicholas Oldisworth, who wrote this book, ... did deliberately read it over, on Thursday the IXth of Oct. 1637, in the hearing of my old grandfather, Sir Nicholas Overbury who affirmed the truth of its contents'. Nicholas Overbury was Thomas Overbury's father.

Rimbault, Ll.D., Edward F. (ed.), *The Miscellaneous Works in Prose and Verse of Sir Thomas Overbury Knt., Now First Collected* (London, John Russell Smith, 1856).

Sawyer, Edmund, *Memorials of Affairs of State in the Reign of Q Elizabeth and K James I Collected (chiefly) from the Original Papers of Sir R. Winwood* (Printed by W. B. for T. Ward, 1725).

Snow, Vernon F., *Essex the Rebel* (Lincoln, University of Nebraska Press, 1970).

Somerset, Anne, *Unnatural Murder: Poison in the Court of King James I* (London, Weidenfeld & Nicolson, 1997).

Sparke, Michael, *The Narrative History of King James for the First Fourteen Years* (London, Michael Sparke, 1651).

Spedding, James, *The Works of Francis Bacon, Baron of Verulam, Viscount St Albans and Lord High Chancellor of England,* collected and edited by James Spedding, Robert Leslie Ellis and Douglas Denon Heath (London, W. Baines and Son, 1824).

Spedding, James (ed.) *Review of the evidence respecting the conduct of King James I in the case of Sir Thomas Overbury* (*Archeologia*, Vol. XLI, Part 1, 1867).

Weldon, Sir Anthony (attrib.), *The Court and Character of King James I* (1650). Reprinted, along with an 'answer', in *The Secret History of the Court of James I*, Sir Walter Scott (ed.) (J. Ballantyne, 1811). This controversial work claims to have been 'written and taken by Sir A.W., being an eye and ear witness'. Shortly after publication its authorship was attributed to Sir Anthony Weldon (1583–1648). Weldon had been clerk of the kitchen and clerk of green cloth to both Elizabeth and James until his dismissal for publishing anti-Scottish views, and *The Court and Character* has been dismissed by some as the sour comments of an aggrieved office holder. The better view is probably that of Edward Rimbault, the editor of Overbury's collected works, who rejected the 'embittered courtier' story and asserted that 'recent discoveries fully confirm the truth of his statements'.

White, Beatrice, *Cast of Ravens: The Strange Case of Sir Thomas Overbury* (London, J. Murray, 1965).

Wilson, Arthur, *History of Great Britain, Being the Life and Reign of King James I* (Richard Lownds, 1653). Wilson, who became steward to the Earl of Essex in 1614, is not generally regarded as an impartial observer, but he nevertheless has much to offer.

INDEX

Abbot, George, *see* CANTERBURY, ARCHBISHOP OF

Anne of Denmark, Queen

    death 195

    friendship with Anne Turner, *see* TURNER, ANNE

    hatred of Overbury 31, 37, 38

    marriage to James VI and I 20, 30-2

        resentments 30-2

    sons Henry and Charles, *see* STUART, HOUSE OF

Annulment of marriage (Frances and Earl of Essex) 42-3, 65-71

    adjournments 67-8, 71

    Answer 66

    facilitation 'plot' by Northampton and Carr 182

    James' involvement in 68-9, 71, 72

    Overbury's refusal to agree to 43-4, 179

        'apology' to Frances 59

        murder by Frances, reason for 181-2

        refusal to withdraw when in Tower 52, 57

    Petition 65, 66-7

    verdict 71-2

    virginity check on Frances for 69-71

Anthony, Francis 190-1

Apothecaries

    fatal enema, giving 83, 98, 175, 187-8

    Franklin, *see* FRANKLIN, JAMES (APOTHECARY)

    de Loubell, Paul, Mayerne's dispenser 144, 146-7, 175

        comments on Overbury's health 184, 185

    Reeve, apothecary's boy 83

Attorney General, *see* BACON, FRANCIS

Aurum potabile

    nature of 190-1

    Overbury taking 191-2, 193

Bacon, Sir Francis 16, 18, 74

    fall from grace after bribes admitted 194

205

faults and strengths 129

homosexuality 20-1

Lord Chancellor and peer 194

trial of Somersets

    addressing court in Carr's trial 140-1

    confession from Carr, seeking 158

    planning approach to trials with James 129-30

    preparation for 129-31

    replacing Coke as in 127

    see also TRIALS AND SENTENCES

unctuous support of Villiers 77

Bright, Robert

coroner 64, 185

Buckingham, *see* VILLIERS, GEORGE

Canterbury, Archbishop of 65 *et seq*

annulment Commission chair 65

    pressure from King for 'correct' verdict 68-9, 71, 76

embassy offer, agreement to 46

Carr, Robert

character 197

court of James I, favourite in 11-15

    Coke's investigation, effect on relationship 89-91

    early gifts and titles received 13-14

    effect of love for Frances on court work 41

falling out over Villiers 77-9

letters from James over Villiers 79-80

relationship with the King established 19

death 156, 195

family background 4-5

Frances (née Howard), Countess of Essex, and 35-6

    daughter with 124, 195

    marriage with 72, 73, 75

    returning her affections 35

    'smitten with her' 40-1

    start of relationship with 29-30

Henry Prince of Wales, whether had hand in death of 176-7

illegal warrant, issue to recover Northampton correspondence 92, 123

    referred to at his trial 146, 150

investigation by Bacon

    'cogitation' upon evidence, allowed opportunities for 130

    innocence protested 131-3

investigation by Coke

    availability for questioning 123

    covering tracks prior to 91-2

    Ellesmere's appointment, seeking to reverse 89, 90

    interrogation 123-4

    King's feelings about 90-1

Index

marriage, first 20

marriage, second (to Frances) 72, 73, 75

murderer, whether was 162-8

Overbury, and 15-17, 18

    accused in plot to murder Overbury 100-1, *see also* TRIALS AND SENTENCES

    break with 44

    'cozening' discovered by brother-in-law 60

    duplicity of Carr over embassy offer 47, 101, 142, 144, 148, 162

    first meeting with 4

    investigation of involvement in his death, *see* COKE, SIR EDWARD

    letters from Tower of London 51, 52, 55-6, 60-2

    murder verdict, whether true 162-8, 180-1, 197

    nature of relationship 18

    powders sent to Tower 53-4

    reliance on 16-17, 38

pardon of 154, 198

Roman Catholic sympathiser 128

Royal Pardon, precautionary application for 80-1, 165

Secretary, acting as, after death of Salisbury 38

Somerset, Earl of, becoming 31n, 72

Tower, in

    leaving 155

    liberty of, granted 154-5

    'threatening' message to James from 172-3

    thrown in before trial 123

    trial of, *see* TRIALS AND SENTENCES

    unpopularity 76

    Villiers becoming King's favourite, effect on 77, 78-81

        King James' responses 78-80

Cecil, Sir Robert 4, 5

    death 38

    Overbury in affections of 16

Charles Stuart, *see* STUART, HOUSE OF

Clare, Earl of, *see* HOLLES, SIR JOHN

Coke, Sir Edward

    dismissal from Bench 194

    investigation of Overbury's death, *see* INVESTIGATION BY COKE

    investigator, prosecutor and judge, as 99, 157

    judge at trials, becoming 99

    removal from post 120, 127-9

    Roman Catholic conspiracy theory 109, 115-16, 120, 169

    trials, judge in, *see* TRIALS AND SENTENCES

Compton Scorpion (or Scorfen)

    birthplace of Overbury 3

Conspiracy theories

    Prince Henry's death, involving 120, 129, 175-8

207

Passion, Poison and Power

Spain and Popish plot, involving

Coke's suspicions 109, 115-16, 128, 169

Franklin begetting 169

Cotton, Sir Robert 92, 124, 128, 143, 150, 151

Court of James I

see also JAMES VI AND I, KING

descriptions of 24-5

Crew, Sir Randolph (Serjeant at law)

trials, at 98, 140, 145

'Cunning Mary', *see* WOODS, MARY

Devereux family

fortunes under Elizabeth I and James I 22

Howards, ill-feeling between 22

Robert, Third Earl of Essex 22

Robert, Fourth Earl of Essex 22

annulment of marriage to Frances, *see* ANNULMENT OF MARRIAGE (FRANCES AND EARL OF ESSEX)

Captain General of Parliamentary army 195

Grand Tour, and return from 24, 26

marriage to Frances Howard 22-3, 26-7

remarriage in 1630 195

trial of Carr, present at 139

trial of Frances, present at 134

Digges, Sir Dudley 47, 144, 160

Doctors

Anthony, Francis, quack physician 190-1

dispensers for, *see* APOTHECARIES

Franklin, self-declared, *see* FRANKLIN, JAMES (APOTHECARY)

Naismith, James 37, 56

Royal physician, *see* DE MAYERNE

Donne, John

Eclogue 74

Elizabeth I, Queen

death 5

Devereux (Third Earl of Essex), and 22

discrimination against Catholics 6

Ellesmere, Lord 89, 90, 134

Elwes, Sir Gervase

Lieutenant of Tower, as 49-50

action after Overbury's death 62-4

'apology' as to Overbury's death 83-6

dismissal and house arrest of 104

reports on Overbury 52, 53, 57-8

suspicions as to poisoning of Overbury revealed 82-3

murder of Overbury, and

confession, implicating Carr 159

role in 196

trial and death of, *see* TRIALS

208

Index

AND SENTENCES

Embassy offer to Overbury

approval of 65

duplicity of Carr over 47, 101, 142, 144, 148, 162

plan for 45, 46-8

Overbury turning down 46-7, 101, 142

Essex, *see* DEVEREUX FAMILY

Evidence

Coke gathering, *see* INVESTIGATION BY COKE

trials, in

hearsay and double hearsay 159-60

selective and partial 159

Executions, *see* TRIALS AND SENTENCES

Forman, Simon

death 35

Frances (Countess of Essex), and

letter from 34

supplying love potions for 34-6

reputation and purported powers 33

Frances (née Howard), *see* HOWARD FAMILY

Franklin, James (apothecary)

administering to Overbury in Tower 84-5, 86

character and looks 95

confession 95-6, 159-60

conspiracy theory 169

liar, known as 95, 164, 169

questioning of 86, 94-7

smothering Overbury, theory 193, 198

statement

Carr's guilt, of 159, 160, 164

Carr's trial, read at 145

summary of confession 95-6, 159-60

trial and death of, *see* TRIALS AND SENTENCES

Gold, drinkable 190-2

Gunpowder Plot 6

Hay, James 125

Helwyss, Sir Gervase, *see* ELWES, SIR GERVASE **49**

Henry Frederick Stuart (Prince of Wales), *see* STUART, HOUSE OF

Herbert, Philip

Earl of Montgomery, created 19

King James' infatuation with 12, 19

marriage 20

Herbert, William (Earl of Pembroke) 42, 76

Holles, Sir John 103, 187n, 188n

Howard family

Catholic sympathisers 21, 39, 76

Frances (Countess of Essex, later Countess of Somerset)

accused in plot to murder Overbury 100-1, *see also*

209

TRIALS AND SENTENCES

annulment of marriage to Essex, *see* ANNULMENT OF MARRIAGE (FRANCES AND EARL OF ESSEX)

Carr, relationship with/subsequent marriage to, *see* CARR, ROBERT

contemporaneous portrayal of 196

daughter, Anne 124, 195

death 155, 195

entry to court 24-5

friends, *see* FORMAN, SIMON; TURNER, ANNE; WOODS, MARY

great-uncle, *see* NORTHAMPTON, FIRST EARL

Henry Frederick Stuart attracted to 27-8

marriage to Robert Carr (Earl of Somerset) 72, 73, 75

marriage to Robert Devereux, *see* DEVEREUX FAMILY

murder of Overbury, part in 52, 57, 185-9

Overbury's death, wish for 44-5, 180

pardon of 154, 198

parents 22

poisoned food to Overbury in Tower 52, 57

pregnancy saving her temporarily from Tower 123

questioning of 124

referred to at his trial 146, 150

Tower, in 124, 134, 154

Tower, leaving 155

trial of, *see* TRIALS AND SENTENCES

Henry (brother of Frances) 35

Henry (great uncle to Frances), *see* NORTHAMPTON, FIRST EARL

power of 21-2

Thomas (Earl of Suffolk)

correspondence with Overbury in Tower 58, 59

corruption, he and wife convicted of 194

Lord Chamberlain, made 74-5

Monson's trial, letter to court 119

Overbury's freedom, intervening for 57

support of James 22

wars with Spain, distinguished in 21-2

wife (Frances' mother) 22

Hyde, Lawrence

prosecutor in trials 100, 102-3, 105, 119

Investigation by Coke 86-88, 96-7

additional support for 89

Carr, of

Coke telling King James of his involvement 88-9

indictment as accessory to murder 126-7

King James' persuasions to

Index

admit guilt 125-6

Tower, incarceration in 123

trial of Carr resulting, *see* TRIALS AND SENTENCES

examinations, zeal in 96-7

Frances, of 123 *et seq*

confession 126

indictment as accessory to murder 126

King James' letter asking her to confess 126

Tower, incarceration in 124

trial of Frances resulting, *see* TRIALS AND SENTENCES

questioning methods available to 158

summary of Franklin's statement 95-6

trials, judge in, *see* TRIALS AND SENTENCES

Weston, examination of 87-8

James VI and I, King

accession to English throne 5-7

affair with Anne Murray 20, 30

annulment of Essex marriage, involvement in 68-9, 71, 72

Buckingham, and, *see* VILLIERS, GEORGE

Carr, relationship with

favourite of 11-15

'friendship not to stand in way of justice' after murder 91, 129-31, 197-8

letter to Carr over Villiers 77-9

see also CARR, ROBERT

character and background 7-11

complex character 197-8

modern views on him 9-10

mother (Mary Queen of Scots) 6, 8-9

death 156, 195

burial place 198

dissolutions of Parliament 39

Esmé Stuart, affection for 4, 10, 19, 20

fear of revelations 174

homosexual relations, whether had 20-1, 153, 197

investigation of Carr and Frances, involvement in 125-6

marriage and children 20, 30, *see also* STUART, HOUSE OF

wife, Anne of Denmark, *see* ANNE OF DENMARK, QUEEN

Overbury, and

'close confinement' ordered in Tower 50-1, 171

early days and honours given 15-19

tired of him 167, 170-1

Roman Catholic leanings 21

'Scottification' by 6-7

son Henry's death, rumours of involvement in 177-8

Villiers, favourite of, *see* VILLIERS,

211

GEORGE

vindictive streak, whether had 171-2

Jonson, Ben 17, 23, 73, 74

Judges at trials 98, 99, 134, 139

Kerr, Robert, *see* CARR, ROBERT

Killigrew, Sir Robert 51

Knyvett, Katherine 22

Knyvett, Sir Thomas 190

Lidcote, Sir John

Overbury's brother-in-law, involvement as

aurum potabile, report that he took 191

visiting in Tower 51, 60

viewing body 62-3

Weston's hanging, conduct at 103-4

Lord Chancellor

Bacon 194

Ellesmere, *see* ELLESMERE, LORD

Lord Chief Justice, *see* COKE, SIR EDWARD

Losely Papers archive 167

de Loubell, Paul, *see* APOTHECARIES

Mainwaring, Sir Arthur

living with Anne Turner 32

Mary Queen of Scots 6, 8-9

Masques

marriage of Frances Howard, to celebrate

Robert Carr, with 73, 74

Robert Devereux, with 22-3

de Mayerne, Theodore

background 55

Carr, attending 12

death 195

dispenser, de Loubell 144, 146-7, 175

King James' personal physician 12, 33, 55

Overbury

attending in Tower 55, 56

murder, whether implicated in 174-5

Prince of Wales, attending 37

documentation of condition of body on death 178

Mercury

causing Overbury's death, possible hypothesis 192, 193

mercuric chloride 192

mercury clyster, contemporaneous use of 189

mercury sublimate 102, 140, 186, 188

mixed with gold and vinegar (aurum potabile) 190-1

Overbury self-administering 191-2

Merston, Simon 52

Monson, Sir Thomas 84, 102

Elwes' accusation of 84, 110, 113, 122

former employee as go-between

Index

for Frances 52

involvement in Overbury plot, surmises on 122

master of the armoury 50

Roman Catholic recusant 117

status after trial 195, 196

trial and release of, *see* TRIALS AND SENTENCES

Weston, appointed by 50

Montague, Sir Henry

trials, Serjeant at law at 98, 140, 144, 150

Carr sent powders to Overbury, stress on 166

Montgomery, Earl of, *see* HERBERT, PHILIP

More, Sir George 132

Carr's refusal to stand trial, go-between in 138

Lieutenant of Tower (after Elwes) 124

Losely Papers archive 167

Mounson, *see* MONSON, SIR THOMAS

Murder of Overbury

Carr as murderer, considerations 162-8

breach of friendship only 167-8

Franklin's statement as to Carr's guilt 160, 164

Losely Papers archive statement 167

Northampton letters, Carr's efforts to destroy 146, 150, 164

Royal Pardon, relevance of application for 80-1, 165

conspiracy theories, *see* CONSPIRACY THEORIES

doctors, role of 174-5

King James's involvement considered 172-4

methods considered 178 *et seq*

poisoning, *see* MERCURY; POISONS

smothering 192-3, 198

Northampton, Carr and Frances as murderers, theory and holes in 179-81

trials, *see* TRIALS AND SENTENCES

two separate plots theory 181-3

Weston as murderer 98-104, 193, 196

Murder of Prince of Wales, theory of 120, 129, 175-8

Naismith, James (Doctor) 37, 56

Northampton, First Earl

burden of government on, after death of Salisbury 38

character of 28-9

correspondence with Carr, recovery to destroy by Carr 92, 123

Carr's trial, referred to at 146, 150, 164

death 39, 74

escaped justice by dying 196

great-uncle to Frances (née

213

Howard) 27, 28

Overbury, and

    Carr's murder trial, Northampton described at 142

    Elwes' accusation of 110, 113, 122

    embassy plan, possible perpetrator of 45

    hatred of/grievances against 38-9, 180

    letter to Carr about Overbury as prisoner 59-60

    murder of Overbury, role in 179, 180

    receipt of letter from Tower 59

    securing in Tower of London 49-50

Roman Catholic, closet 28-9

wedding gifts to Frances and Robert Carr 73

Overbury, Sir Thomas

    annulment of Essex marriage, objection to 43-4, 179

        'apology' to Frances 59

        refusal to withdraw when in Tower 52, 57

arrest 46-8

birth and early life 3-4

Carr, relationship with, see CARR, ROBERT

character and talents 17-18, 198-9

    described by Bacon at Carr's trial 141-2

    pride 18

court of James I, at 15-19

    first official appointment 15

    King's attitude changing after Villiers on scene 170-1

    knighthood and gift of property 16

    meddling in affairs of state 38

    more involvement as Carr busy with Frances 41

death 62

    burial 62-4

    causes considered 183-93, 198

    coroner called 64

    Elwes' 'apology' 82-3

    investigation of, see COKE, SIR EDWARD

    methods considered 178 *et seq, see also* MERCURY; POISONS

    murder trials, see TRIALS AND SENTENCES

embassy, offer of, see EMBASSY OFFER TO OVERBURY

father, Nicholas 56-7, 195

Henry Prince of Wales, whether hand in death of 177

Howards

    dislike of 38, 43, 45

    Frances (née Howard), dynamics 29-30, 43-5, 180

ill-health 182, 183-4

Index

contributing to his death 184

spleen trouble 46, 184

tuberculosis diagnosis 175, 183-4

murder theories, *see* MURDER OF OVERBURY

poisoning

conspiracy theories, *see* CONSPIRACY THEORIES

investigation of, *see* COKE, SIR EDWARD

murder trials, *see* TRIALS AND SENTENCES

symptoms point to 185-7

theories about 169-78, 181-3

see also MERCURY; POISONS

Queen Anne, makes enemy of 31, 37, 38

Tower of London, incarceration in 46-8

bodily assaults/poisoning 52-4, 57

letters to Carr 51, 52, 55-6, 60-2

letters to Earl of Suffolk 58, 59

letter to Northampton 59

medical treatment 55-6, 167

mental pressure on 52, 57-8

parents' pleas for release 56-7

poisoning and foul play, later evidence of 82-6, *see also* POISONS

rigorous restraints imposed 50-1, 171

two plots theory as to his death 181-3

Payton, Henry

servant to Overbury 44, 47, 142, 144, 184

Poisons

Anne Turner's house, found in, list and properties of 92-4

aqua fortis (nitric acid) 94

cantharides fly 93, 94, 186

Carr, and 54, 144-5, 166

explanation of 148

Montague's stress on 140, 166

role in 165-6

cause of Overbury's death, symptoms point to 185-7

cited in prosecution case against Carr 140

fatal enema ('clyster') story 83, 98, 175, 179, 187-9

Weston's involvement, prosecution version of 103, 187-8

Franklin's statement on 95-6

great spider 93, 186

lapis causticus (potassium hydroxide) 94

mercury/mercury sublimate, *see* MERCURY

rosalgar or realgar (red arsenic) 93, 102, 140, 186

tarts containing, sent to Overbury 88, 104, 186-7

215

white arsenic 93, 140, 186

Raleigh, Sir Walter

Coke's prosecution of 87

manor of Sherborne given to Carr 13, 152

Tower of London, and 51, 86, 125

Rawlins, Giles

manservant to Overbury 53, 91, 140

Reeve, William 83

Rider, Edward 175

Rochester, Viscount

see also Carr, Robert

Carr created 14

Roman Catholics

see also Spain

Carr as sympathiser 128

Coke's idea of conspiracy by 109, 115-16

discrimination against 6

Howards as sympathisers 21, 39, 76

James I, crypto-Catholic 21

Northampton, closet 28-9

Salisbury, Lord, see Cecil, Sir Robert

Simcocks, John 163

Somerset, Earl of, see Carr, Robert

Southampton, Third Earl of, see Wriothesley, Henry

Spain

conspiracy theory involving, and Overbury death

Coke's suspicion of 109, 115-16, 120, 169

Franklin perpetrating rumours 169

issue of 39

pension from

Carr receiving 165

James receiving 39n

Northampton receiving 28

Stuart, House of

Anne of Denmark, Queen, see Anne of Denmark, Queen

Arabella, Lady 171-2

Charles Stuart

dynastic marriage with Spain, Carr seeking 128

heir apparent, becoming 128

King, after James's death 156

Esmé 4, 10, 19, 20

Henry Frederick Stuart (Prince of Wales)

attraction to Frances Howard 27-8

death 36-7, 175, 178

dislike of Carr 177

dislike of Overbury 177

investiture, Masque on 29-30

murder theory and rumours 120, 129, 175-8

James VI of Scotland/I of England, see James VI and I, King

Index

Suffolk, Thomas Earl of, *see* HOWARD FAMILY

Tower of London

    Carr in 123

    Frances in 124

    Overbury in, *see* OVERBURY, THOMAS

Tudor, House of 5, 8

Trials and sentences

    Bacon, replacing Coke as judge 127

        addressing court in Carr's trial 140-1

        Carr's trial, prosecutor at 139

        Carr's petition for mercy, dealing with 146

        preparation for Somerset trials 129-31

    bench 98, 139, *see also* BACON; and 'Coke' *below*

    Carr (Earl of Somerset), of 139-53

        charge 139

        defence 147-51

        fairness of trial of, considerations 156-61

        Franklin's statement as evidence 145

        initial refusal to stand trial 137-8

        letters between Northampton and Carr, illegal warrant for 143-4, 146, 150

        de Loubell, apothecary, non-appearance as witness 144, 146-7

        no counsel or right to call witnesses 159

        pardon given 155

        pardon sought 146, 151

        persuaded by More to attend court 138

        plea 139

        prosecution case 140-7

        reputation besmirched before charge 160-1

        'threat' to King James, whether presented 172-4

        verdict and sentence 151-2

    Coke, judge

        intervention in Carr's trial 146-7

        letter to King James and indiscretions 120

        remarks and outbursts 109, 115, 116-17, 118-19

        removal 120, 127-9

    Elwes, Sir Gervase, of 108-12

        confession, implicating Carr 159

        confession by Franklin, implicated in 95-6, 111-12

        evidence extracted and paraphrased, complaint that 159

        evidence thin but behaviour inexcusable 114

        hanging of 112-13

        verdict 112

Passion, Poison and Power

fairness considered 156-61

Frances, Countess of Somerset, of 134-7

    dependency, in state of 135

    'dumb shew', as 136

    guilty plea 135-6

    pardon given 154

    reputation besmirched before charge made 160-1

    verdict and sentence 136-7

Franklin, James, of 114

    confession (summary of) 95-6, 114-15

    death on gallows 117

    verdict and sentence 115

hearsay evidence, use of 159-60

Monson, Sir Thomas, of 117-22

    discontinuance 120

    letter from Thomas Howard to court 119

    pardon and release from Tower 120-1

    reason for inconclusive end 121-2

prosecution figures

    Hyde, prosecutor 100, 102-3, 105, 119

    Montague 98, 140, 144, 150

    see also 'Bacon'; 'Coke', *above*

Somersets (Carr and Frances), of 134 *et seq*

    adjournments 131

Carr's trial, *see* 'Carr (Earl of Somerset), of' *above*

confession from Carr sought 131-3

Frances' trial, *see* 'Frances (Countess of Somerset), of' *above*

planned approach to 129-31

Turner, Anne, of 105-08

    death 108

    verdict and sentence 107

Weston, Richard, of 98-104

    accusation against Earl and Countess of Somerset in 100-1

    agreeing to trial by jury 102

    confession implicating Carr 159

    evidence thin 104

    hanging of 103

    jury 99

    verdict and sentence 103

Trumbull, William 83

Turner, Anne 32, 74

    arrest pending trial 94, 104

    Carr issuing illegal warrant on 92, 123

    court of James I, description of 23

    friendship with Queen Anne 32-3

    letter from Frances 34

    Mainwaring, Sir Arthur, living with 32

    poisoning of Overbury,

Index

implication in 57, 85, 86

    noxious substances found in her house 92-4

Roman Catholic 107

trial of, *see* TRIALS AND SENTENCES

Villiers, George

assassination of 195

Bacon's letter to, about Frances' trial 136

Baron Whaddon, created 152-3

Buckingham Earldom, elevation to 153

court appointments 77, 78

King James, and

    effect of Villiers supplanting Carr in his affections 167, 170-1

    embarrassment to 155

    favourite of 20, 76-8, 152-3

Knighthood 78

Wade, Sir William 49

Wentworth, Sir John 103

Weston, Richard

encounters between Carr and Frances Essex, arranged 36

gaoler of Overbury in Tower

    appointed by Monson as 50

'clyster' to Overbury, prosecution version of 103, 187-8

'clyster' to Overbury, report to Elwes on 84-5, 188

foiled attempt to poison Overbury, and 53, 84, 87-8, 182-3

questioning of 86, 87

smothering Overbury, theory of 193, 198

tarts sent by Frances, how dealt with 88, 104, 186-7

trial and conviction of 98-104

villain, as 196

Winwood, Sir Ralph 74, 76

Secretary of State, as 82, 83

Wood(es) Sir David 45

Woods, Mary 40-1

Wriothesley, Henry

annulment of Essex marriage, plan for 43

King's hatred for Overbury when in Tower, writing of 171

Southampton, Earl of 43

Yelverton, Sir Henry (Solicitor General) 100

219